Biblical Questions and Answers for Smart Kids

Quizzes Focused on the Book of Exodus to Help Your Children Grow & Learn about God – Who He is, His Love, & His Relationship with Humanity.

Only One Life

Only One Life

Contents

Introduction

This is Book 2 in The Pentateuch Kids' Q&A Series. It is a five-book series, and the focus of this second one is Exodus.

The Bible is a vast book with different topics, teachings, and experiences. Sometimes, people are confused about how to go about reading it, not knowing where to start, and are unsure about knowing some stories well enough. Only One Life is aware of this confusion that the average Christian family faces. I have come up with "focused quizzes" to help solve some of these problems and to help us connect easily with our Maker.

I will ask questions from the Book of Exodus. These quizzes will help individuals or groups grasp a more profound knowledge of the truths in this beautiful book. These are self-scoring interactive quizzes with answers at the back of the book to help you learn and have fun at the same time. You can use these quizzes by yourself or as games with your family, loved ones, or even in church activities. You could arrange people into two or as many parties as you want and follow the quizzes as they come. Try to give yourselves at least 15 seconds between the question and the answer, so you have a little time to think.

The quizzes are multiple choice, fill in the gap, true or false, and some review activities. There are 56 quizzes sectioned into bits sizes to help the kids grasp more from the areas I took the questions from. They are great for youth ministry and can be used for Sunday School lessons, Bible studies, or other activities. I aim to inspire and encourage Christians in their Bible studies, helping them discover the depth of detail within this precious book.

Now you don't have to worry about not having Christian Ethics in schools because this is all from the Bible, and these questions will challenge your child. These Bible quizzes will teach them to know about God—who He is, what He is like, His love for humans, and how we all need Him.

You will notice special questions highlighted with icons scattered throughout this book. I call them "Thinking Outside the Box" questions. They are meant to be more thought. Answers will be more personal and will help connect the dots between other Bible chapters and verses. These "Thinking Outside the Box" questions have no objective answers underneath, but my insight on those questions is provided in the answer key at the back of this book, along with the Bible reference to each answer. Exodus is the bible's second book. The word, "Exodus" is a Hebrew word that signifies "exit" or "departure." The exodus of the children of Israel from Egypt represents the exodus of all the chosen people from the land where they had been slaves for generations. Moses is the author of this Bible book. The birth of Moses, the plagues by which God liberated the Israelites from Egypt, the trek to Sinai, the imparting of the law, and a description of the tabernacle are all revealed in the quizzes.

The New King James Version Bible was used dominantly in writing this book.

We would love to see many other children being taught God's truths in their homes. If we were valuable to you in that way, please leave an honest review on Amazon or your bookstore, and it will encourage other parents to teach their children about God—with our help.

I pray God will give you the spirit of wisdom and revelation in the knowledge of Him, open the eyes of your understanding that you may know the hope of His calling, the riches of His glory, and the greatness of His power towards you according to the working of His power which He worked in Christ when He raised Him from the dead" (Ephesians 1:17-20). In Jesus' name. Amen!

Quiz 1
Read Exodus 1:1-19

1.Towards the end of Genesis, we knew that Jacob, whose name was changed to Israel, took his family to the Land of Egypt. His favorite son, Joseph, was still alive, being second in command to Pharaoh (King of Egypt). We also learned that seventy souls went to Egypt–this includes Joseph and his two Egyptian-born sons. In Egypt, Israel died and was buried in Canaan, according to the command of the Pharaoh. Joseph and his brothers died, as did the generation of Joseph and the ones after. The Egyptian Pharaoh, also, was dead. Israel's children were multiplying because of the promise God gave to their fathers, Abraham, Isaac, and Jacob. They became strong and mighty, even though they were slaves in Egypt. Somebody became afraid of the Hebrews' might and population. Who was fearful of the Children of Israel?

    a. Potiphar
    b. Pharaoh
    c. Egyptian midwives
    d. Egyptian priests

2. In Egypt, a new king (Pharaoh) arose who did not know about Joseph and what he did. He saw the population of the children of Israel, how strong and mighty they were. He became afraid of them and thought they would be bad for Egypt. What did Pharaoh think the Children of Israel would do?

    a. They would rise against his throne.
    b. They would attack them unawares.
    c. They would join forces with their enemies and war against them.
    d. They would marry their young girls.

3. The King of Egypt thought the Children of Israel might revolt, join forces with their enemies and fight against them in

the event of war, so he came up with a plan to do something. What was his plan?

a. They set up instructors to teach them their language and ways.

b. They set up undercover police squads to live amongst them to send their discoveries to Pharaoh and his men.

c. They set up taskmasters over them to afflict them with their burden.

d. They issued them a pill for birth control.

4. Pharoah and his people became afraid of the Israelites' numbers and might, so they set up taskmasters over them to make them work harder. They also made the Children of Israel build things for Pharaoh. What did they ask the Israelites to build?

a. Supply cities, Pithom and Raamses

b. Disney city, supply cities, and Raamses

c. Restaurants, supply cities, and worship centers

d. Libraries, supply cities, and warehouses

5. Pharoah and his people made the Israelites labor with hard bondage. They made bricks and built the supply cities of Pithom and Raamses, yet the Children of Israel were still multiplying and getting stronger. Pharoah was still afraid and devised another means to deal with his slave enemies—the Israelites. He told the Israelite midwives to do something to keep their numbers down. What did he tell them?

a. He asked them to throw all the boy babies into the river.

b. He asked them to circumcise all the boy babies.

c. He asked them to kill all the girl babies.

d. He asked them to kill all the boy babies.

6. Pharoah talked to two midwives. Is that true or false?

7. Pharaoh told the two midwives to kill the Hebrew baby boys. The two midwives were _____.

a. Shiphrah and Puah

b. Hannah and Puah

c. Puah and Hannah

d. Shiphrah and Hannah

8. Who was the first person to be called a Hebrew?

9. The midwives disobeyed Pharaoh by not killing the boy babies. Why?
a. Because they loved children
b. Because the parents of the children paid them
c. Because they identified with the Hebrew women
d. Because they feared God

10. The midwives feared God and refused to obey what Pharaoh had asked them to do. Pharaoh was unhappy, so he asked them why they hadn't done as he had asked them to. What did they tell Pharoah?
a. They said the Israelite men were always with the women when they gave birth and because they were stronger than them, they quickly took the boy babies from them.
b. They said the Israelite men decided to be midwives for their wives.
c. They said the Israelite women were not like the Egyptian women because they were lively and gave birth before they could get there.
d. They said they could not be a part of Pharaoh's horrible plan for the Israelites.

Summary

Phew! That was a lot to take in, wasn't it? Pharaoh, the king of Egypt, was afraid of his slaves and sought every opportunity to bring their numbers down. Have you tried to think about why some people are bullies? Well, I think it's because they are fearful like Pharoah. He tried every means to stop the Children of Israel from growing, but you know what? Nobody can stop the plan God has for you, only you can. How can you stop God's plans for yourself? By not believing in the promises He has given to you.

Once you believe what the Bible says about you, no nothing can stop you.

Again, we saw the two midwives that disobeyed their king, Pharaoh. If you were one of the midwives, what would you have done? Would you have killed innocent babies or put it in more modern terms, if your friend asked you to play a dangerous prank on someone else, will you do it?

Note: The Children of Isreal, Israelites, and Hebrews are all referring to the same people. I used those names interchangeably so you can get familiar with them.

Quiz 2
Read Exodus 1:20-22; 2:1-3, 6:20.

1.The two midwives told Pharaoh that the Israelite women were not like the Egyptians because they were lively and gave birth before they could get there. That was why they could not kill the boy babies. Because these midwives feared God and refused to kill the boy babies, God did something for them. What did He do for the midwives?
   a. He provided food for them.
   b. He provided chariots for them.
   c. He provided lands for them.
   d. He provided households for them.

2. Pharaoh became disappointed with the midwives' actions, so he commanded his people to do something to the Israelites' boy babies. What did he ask his people to do?
   a. He asked them to cut off the neck of every male baby.
   b. He asked them to pierce the heart of every male baby.
   c. He asked them to throw every male baby into the river.
   d. He asked them to cover the nose of every male baby so they would die when they could not breathe.

3. One woman had a baby boy and hid him from Pharoah's evil men during this time. What was the name of this lady?
   a. Hannah
   b. Rebekah
   c. Deborah
   d. Jochebed

4. Jochebed's husband was _____.
   a. Abram
   b. Judah
   c. Levi

d. Amram

5. Jochebed and Amram came from the tribe of Judah. Is that true or false?

6. Israel's name was first given to one person. Who was it first given to?

7. Jochebed had her baby boy, and she somehow knew the child was unique. What did she know?
a. She knew the child was a hero.
b. She knew the child was beautiful.
c. She knew the child was going to live in the palace.
d. She knew the child was going to be a troublemaker.

8. Jochebed knew her baby was unique, so she hid him from Pharaoh's men. How long did she conceal her baby?
a. Two months
b. Three months
c. Four months
d. Five months

9. Jochebed and Amram had a daughter named Mia. Is that true or false?

10. Jochebed and Amram had a son older than Moses. What is the name of that son?
a. Aaron
b. Joshua
c. Hur
d. Nimrod

Summary

The two midwives gave Pharaoh their made-up reason for not killing the babies. Pharaoh was not happy, and he issued a throw-every-boy-baby-in-the-river decree.

We also saw a mother who saw her son to be beautiful that disobeyed Pharoah's decree for a moment. Do not forget that Moses's mom and dad are from the tribe of Levi. Levi is the third son of Jacob (Israel) he had with Leah (Genesis 29:34.)

Quiz 3
Read Exodus 2:4-8.

1. Jochebed kept her baby boy hidden for three months. When she could no longer hide him, she made an ark of bulrushes to keep him. Is that true or false?

2. Jochebed took the ark of bulrushes and used something to make its finishing. What did she use?
   a. She daubed it with asphalt and pitch.
   b. She painted it to pitch and blue.
   c. painted it blue and brown.
   d. She painted it grey and pitch.

3. When Jochebed could no longer hide her baby, she took an ark of bulrushes, daubed it with asphalt and pitch, then put her baby inside and placed the ark _____ by the riverbank.
   a. In a canoe
   b. On the sand
   c. Under a tree
   d. In the reeds

4. Jochebed placed her baby in the ark and kept it in the reeds by the riverbank. Her daughter, Miriam, stood and waited to see _____.
   a. Who will find the ark
   b. Who will open the ark first
   c. What would happen to her baby brother
   d. How crocodiles will eat her baby brother

5. When the ark was in the reeds, someone came to the river. Who went to the riverbank?
   a. The daughter of an Israelite leader

b. The daughter of Pharaoh
c. The son of Pharaoh
d.The son of an Israelite leader

6. Pharaoh's daughter came to the river bank to do something. What did she come to do?
a. She came to worship their god.
b. She came to fetch water.
c. She came to bathe.
d. She came to sacrifice to the river goddess.

7. Pharaoh's daughter did not come to the riverbank alone. She came with her bodyguards. Is that true or false?

8. Pharaoh's daughter and her maids came to bathe in the river. They saw the ark, opened it up, and saw the child doing something. What was the baby doing?
a. He was sucking his finger.
b. He was cooing.
c. He was sleeping.
d. He was crying.

9. When Pharoah's daughter saw the baby inside the ark crying, she had compassion for him, saying, "This is one of the Hebrew children" Exodus 2:6. The baby's sister was watching, so she went to meet Pharaoh's daughter and asked her a question. What was her question?
a. Should I be the babysitter?
b. Should I call his mom for you?
c. Should I find a Hebrew woman to nurse him for you?
d. Should I bring his clothes for you?

10. The baby's sister asked Pharaoh's daughter if she could bring a Hebrew woman to nurse the child for her. Pharaoh's daughter said, "Go." The baby's sister went to call someone for Pharaoh's daughter. Who did she call?
a. She went to call one midwife.
b. She went to call a Hebrew woman that had just given birth.
c. She went to call the baby's aunt.
d. She went to call the baby's mom, who was also her mom.

Different Opinions

In reading this story, some people will see coincidence while others will see a miracle (hand of God at work). Why does it have to be that Pharaoh's daughter was the first person to go to the river bank when the baby was kept there? Have you thought about that? Well, it could have been Pharaoh himself, or some other hateful people at that sport when baby Moses was kept there. Think about it for a moment.

What about your existence? What do you see around you? Coincidence, luck, or God at work? You are no coincidence. You are the handiwork of God!

Quiz 4
Read Exodus 2:9-16.

1.The baby's mother appeared before Pharaoh's daughter, who asked her to nurse the child and that she would give her something. What did she say she would give the child's mom?
   a. Wages
   b. A house
   c. A chariot
   d. Maidens

2. The baby's mother took her son and nursed him for wages. When the baby grew, she brought him to Pharaoh's daughter, who named the child. What did Pharaoh's daughter call the child?
   a. Amram
   b. Benji
   c. Samson
   d. Moses

3. The first child tax benefit in the Bible was paid to who?

4. Moses became a grown man while living in the palace. One day, he visited the Israelites, his people, to see how they were treated. When he arrived, he saw an Egyptian beating an Israelite. No one was watching him, so he did something. What did he do?
   a. He killed the Israelites and the Egyptians and buried them in the sand.
   b. He killed the Egyptian person and buried him in the sand.

c. He whipped the two of them, even if it was a crime to flog an Egyptian.

d. He blinded the eyes of the Egyptian.

5. Moses went out to see his people on the second day, and something happened. What was it?

a. He saw two Israelites eating an unhealthy meal.

b. He saw two Egyptians beating up an Israelite.

c. He saw Egyptian and Israelite planning to hurt an Israelite.

d. He saw two Israelites fighting.

6. When Moses saw the two Israelites fighting, he told them to stop fighting because they were brothers. The one in the wrong asked Moses questions. What were the questions he asked him?

a. Why are you a prince and a judge? Do you want to take me to Pharoah?

b. Are you a prince and a judge? Didn't you see anything reasonable to do?

c. Who made you a prince and a judge? Do you want to kill me the way you killed the Egyptian the other day?

d. Who said you are a prince and a judge? Do you want to come and live in Raamses?

7. How old was Moses when he ran away from Egypt?

a. Fifty years

b. Forty-five years

c. Forty years

d. Thirty-eight years

8. Moses was scared when he heard the questions one of the fighting Israelites asked him. He reasoned it wouldn't be long before Pharaoh came for him since the people knew about it. When Pharaoh discovered what Moses had done, he sought to kill him. Moses fled and ran off through the desert into a different country. Which country did Moses run to?

a. Midian

b. Ethiopia

c. Libya

d. The country of the East

9. When Moses arrived in Midian, he was tired, having nowhere to go. He sat by a pond. Is that true or false?

10. The priest of Midian had several daughters that came to draw water from the well Moses was sitting by. How many daughters did the Midianite priest have?
a. Five
b. Six
c. Seven
d. Eight

Choose!

How are you doing so far? Go ahead and congratulate yourself. Actually, you're doing great. If you missed a few, don't worry, but you also don't have to give up. Read the Bible verse and answer the questions. You will quickly make meaningful progress. Do you realize everyone began where you are now? You will learn more about what is in the Bible as you read and listen more. Good job!

A full-grown Moses identified with his people-Israelites. He has every right to be identified with the Egyptians, for he grew up in the palace as a prince, but he identifies with the people of God who were slaves at the moment. If you were Moses, which people would you have identified with? A prince (Egyptian) or a slave (Hebrew)? Okay, you are not Moses, and you probably know the story very well, so you identified with the Hebrews. But, do you know you can choose to be the modern-day Moses? In your school, sport, etc., do you call yourself a Christian (a child of God) when you know people will mock you? Do you choose to stand for the truth even when it will cost you your friends, love, care, and popularity? Think about it. You can choose to be a modern-day Moses or be an evil prince. Take your pick.

Circle anything that was mentioned in saving baby Moses and X every other.

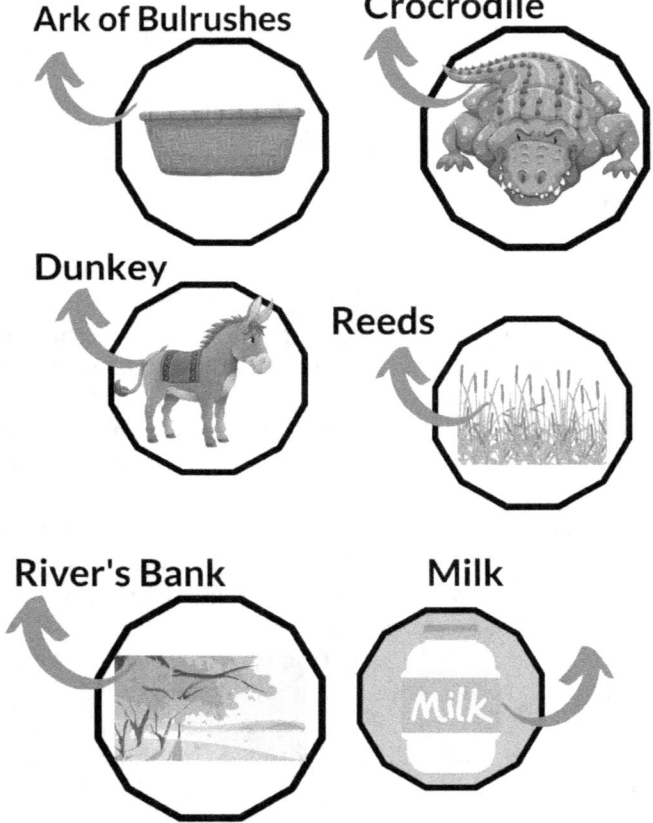

Ark of Bulrushes

Crocrodile

Dunkey

Reeds

River's Bank

Milk

Quiz 5
Read Exodus 2:16-23, 18:4

1.The priest's seven daughters came to draw water from the well Moses was sitting beside. Some bully shepherds came to drive them away, but Moses _____.

    a. Threatened them

    b. Stood up for the seven sisters, helped them, and then watered their flock

    c. Fainted to deceive the shepherd.

    d. Called for backup from the priest of Midian

2. The priest of Midian's name was Lamech. Is that true or false?

3. Reuel's seven daughters told him of the man that had helped them. He asked for Moses. Why did Reuel send for Moses?

    a. That he might take a bath

    b. That he might eat bread

    c. That he can marry one of his daughters

    d. That he may tell him, "Thank you."

4. Moses stayed in Reuel's home. Reuel gave Moses one of his daughters to be his wife. Who did Moses marry?

    a. Mahalalel

    b. Messabage

    c. Zipporah

    d. Albamaneh

5. Ruel, Zipporah's father, was a priest of the Most High God, and he wasn't a Jew. This means that God's relationship with men in the Old Testament wasn't limited to the Jews alone. Balaam was not a Jew either, yet God spoke to him, and He even made his donkey speak to him (Numbers 22). There is another confirmation of this claim in Genesis. We talked about it in the Genesis series of this book. The priest in Genesis 14:18-24 was also a king, and he was the one Abram paid tithes to. What is the name of this priest?

6. Moses and Zipporah had _ _ _ _ _ sons?
a. Two
b. Three
c. Four
d. Five

7. The name of Moses and Zipporah's first son was Samson. Is that true or false?

8. What is the meaning of Gershom?
a. God has remembered me
b. Stranger here
c. God has made me forget my sorrows
d. God is good

9. Their second son's name was _ _ _ _ _ _.
a. Eliezer
b. Semion
c. Heman
d. Ephraim

10. While Moses was in Midian, what happened to the Pharaoh in Egypt?
a. He became sick.
b. He died.
c. He went overseas.
d. He had an accident.

Can you copycat Moses?

Injustice! Injustice!! Injustice!!!

Moses hated that word, injustice. Sometimes I would ask myself, can't he learn his lesson? Other times, I would try to copycat him. I think every child of God should hate injustice or anything that is evil. Do you remember why Moses fled to Midian? It's on quiz 4. He saw an Egyptian beating up an Israelite. Moses said to himself, 'I will not stay here and watch this wrongdoing.' So he killed the Egyptian and buried him. He ran away because of that crime and now, he saw bully shepherds bullying the seven shepherdesses of Jethro, the Priest of Midian. He couldn't contain himself and stood for them. I think Moses had a very good heart that loves God and hates evil. Would you try to fight against evil like him? When I say evil here, I mean lies, ungodly pranks, disobedience to parents and authority, bullying your younger ones, etc. Well..., will ya?

Quiz 6
Read Exodus 2:24-35; 3:1-5.

1. The new pharaoh in Egypt was harsher, and the Israelites were suffering more than before. They cried to God, who heard their voice and remembered _____.
   a. His covenant with Abraham, Isaac, and Jacob
   b. His covenant with Moses and Reuel
   c. His promise to Reuel and the people of Midian
   d. His promise to Noah

2. At Midian, Moses was a shepherd. Is that true or false?

3. At Midian, Moses became a shepherd. The sheep he was looking after belonged to who?
   a. His sheep
   b. His wife, Zipporah's sheep
   c. His father-in-law, Reuel's sheep
   d. His neighbor, Salmon's sheep

4. Moses' father-in-law, Reuel, had a different name. What was his other name?
   a. Reuelnelah
   b. Jethro
   c. Johnson
   d. Molalah

5. One day, Moses led Jethro's sheep to the desert and came to a mountain. What was the name of that mountain?
   a. Horeb
   b. Sanai
   c. Gilead
   d. Gestamine

6. What is another name for Mount Horeb?
a. The Mountain of God
b. The Mountain of the Misery
c. The Mountain of the Salute
d. The Mountain of Terror

7. At the mountain, an angel of the Lord appeared to Moses as a man. Is that true or false?

8. Moses led Reuel's sheep to Horeb, the Mountain of God. In a blaze of fire, the Lord's angel appeared to him. Where was the fire burning?
a. On the grass
b. On a tree
c. In a bush
d. On a rock

9. Moses looked at the fire burning, but it did not consume the bush. He wondered why the bush was on fire but not burning up. When he tried moving closer, God called him from the bush and talked to him. What did God tell Moses?
a. Do not draw near this place, so I will not consume you.
b. Do not draw near this place. Otherwise, you will turn into a burning bush.
c. Do not draw near this place because I have made you holy.
d. Do not draw near this place. Take off your sandals from your feet, for the place you are standing on is holy ground.

10. Moses became a shepherd looking after his father-in-law's sheep. We know Moses grew up in the palace, and he was "Learned in all the wisdom of the Egyptians and was mighty in words and deeds," as stated in Acts 7:22. Since Moses had the education of the Egyptians, they trained him to hate his current job - shepherd, because we learned in our first book of Genesis that "... Every shepherd is _ _ _ _ _" Genesis 46:34.

God's Creation!

Hum..., curious Moses. He saw the bush burning, and he drew closer to see what was going on. Do you act like that sometimes? Are you kidding me? I know you do. I do, too. Everyone does! The question is, what things are you curious about? In case you don't know, just as God revealed Himself to Moses in the burning bush, He is revealing Himself to us every day. The problem with us is that we don't seem to see Him because we are too busy being curious about other things. Other times, even when we see Him, we ignore Him. Oh, you are wondering how I knew He is showing Himself to us today? The Bible, of course. He also shows Himself in practically everything around us. Psalm 19:1-3 says, "The heavens declare the glory of God; And the firmament shows His handiwork. Day unto day utters speech, And night unto night reveals knowledge. There is no speech nor language, where their voice is not heard." Do you look at the skyline sometime? Do you look at those gophers jumping and digging holes everywhere? What about the flowers, grass, and trees in your yard? Do you try to ask the why, how, when, etc. of those trees and see the glory of God in them? Day and night, 24/7, God's creation is speaking forth His glory. The witness of creation is heard in every language on earth, as verse 3 of Psalm 19 said. God's creation is loudly and clearly proclaiming the existence and glory of God. I challenge you to look for God in everything. You will find Him, I'm certain.

Quiz 7
Read Exodus 3:6-22; 4:1-6.

1.God told Moses not to draw closer, and that he should take off his shoes because he was standing on holy ground. After that, what did God do?

a. He introduced Himself to Moses.

b. He gave Moses rules.

c. He rebuked Moses for not being patient, running away from Egypt, and leaving his people to suffer.

d. He gave Moses a vision of the future.

2. God told Moses that He is the God of Abraham, Isaac, and Jacob. He said He had seen and heard the cry of His people in Egypt, and He had come to deliver them from their bondage. Moses must have been happy to hear that. What else did God say to Moses?

a. He wants to bring them to the Red Sea.

b. He wants to bring them to the land He had promised their fathers–the land flowing with milk and honey.

c. He wants to test the Israelites to see if they believe in Him.

d. He wants the Israelites to wage war against Pharaoh and his people.

3. God told Moses that the Canaanites, Hittites, Amorites, Perizzites, Hivites, and Jebusites lived in the land He had promised their fathers. What else did He tell Moses?

a. I will drive away all the people I have mentioned away from the land before you arrive there.

b. I will take the Israelites out of Egypt by force. Nothing is too hard for me, for I am God.

c. I have seen how Pharaoh is oppressing My children, and I want to send you to him, and you will bring My people, the Children of Israel, out of Egypt.

d. I want you to know that I have chosen you.

4. Whoa! Moses must have been surprised because he thought he could not meet Pharaoh and bring God's people out, but God assured Moses that He would be with him. He gave Moses one of the following assurances. Which one did God give him?

a. When you get to Egypt, Aaron shall meet you at the gate and hug you.

b. You shall serve me on this mountain when you have brought Israel out of Egypt.

c. The rainbow will stretch across the sky before you enter Egypt.

d. Your wife, Zipporah, shall go with you into Egypt.

5. Moses did not know the name of God at this time other than the God of Abraham, Isaac, and Jacob or the God of your fathers. He was worried the people might ask him to tell them the name of the God that sent him. When he asked God His name, God told him His name. What is the name God gave Moses?

a. I Am the Creator.

b. I Am the God of Abraham, Isaac, and Jacob.

c. I AM Who I Am.

d. I Am the Almighty God.

6. God told Moses that He should gather the elders of Israel and tell them I AM had sent him to them. He also asked him to say that He is the God of their father, Abraham, Isaac, and Jacob. God said that was His name forever, and His memorial to all generations. God told Moses to also tell the Israelites that He had heard their voice and will bring them to the land He had promised their fathers–the land of the Canaanites, Hittites, Amorites, Perizzites, Hivites, and Jebusites. He assured Moses that His people would listen to him. Moses was to tell Pharaoh that the God of the Hebrews had met with them and he should please let them go into the wilderness so they might sacrifice to their God. How many days will they need to go into the wilderness before they sacrifice?

a. Two days

b. Three days

c. Four days

d. Five days

7. God told Moses to tell Pharoah they would go on a three-day journey into the wilderness to offer sacrifice to their God, but Pharaoh would disagree. God would then strike Egypt with His wonders. After that, they would go. God would give them favor before the Egyptians, and every woman would ask their neighbor to give them _____ for their journey.

a. Articles of silver, articles of gold, and clothing
b. Articles of bronze, articles of gold, and livestock
c. Articles of silver, articles of gold, and livestock
d. Articles of gold, articles of diamonds, and silver

8. Moses was still in doubt and asked God what would happen if Pharaoh did not believe him. In Moses' hand was a rod, and God asked him to put it down. What happened to the rod when Moses set it on the ground?

a. It changed to a golden ring.
b. It changed to a staff with a horn.
c. It changed to a crocodile.
d. It changed to a snake/serpent.

9. Moses dropped the rod in his hand, and it turned into a serpent. God asked him to pick the snake up by the neck. Is that true or false?

10. The Lord also told Moses to put his hand under his armpit. When he did, something happened to his hand. What happened to Moses' hand?

a. His hand turned to gold.
b. His hand became renewed.
c. His hand turned to the hand of a baby.
d. His hand became leprous, like snow.

Look for God!

Moses looked for God, and he found Him. That corresponds with what the Bible said in Jeremiah 29:13 "And you will seek Me and find Me, when you search for Me with all your heart." You know, God is everywhere. Are you seeing Him right where you are? If you are not, that means you are not looking for Him. He said we will find Him when we look for Him with all our hearts. You don't pretend about this at all. You have to be sincere with yourself. Moses sought and found God and He introduced Himself to him. Wonderful! God wants to show Himself to you the way you have not known Him before. I am curious to know one way He revealed Himself to you, so if you can let me know at onlyonelifestory.co m, that would be great.

Quiz 8
Read Exodus 4:7-20.

1.God asked Moses to put his leprous hand back under his armpit, and it returned to normal when he did. Then God told him that if the Israelites did not believe the first sign he showed them, they would believe the second. After Moses had shown the Hebrews the two signs, if they did not believe, then Moses would take water from the river and pour it onto the dry land. What did God say the water would turn to?
   a. Oil
   b. Blood
   c. Wine
   d. Snow

2. God said to Moses, "Go, return to Egypt, for all the men who sought your life are dead" (Exodus 4:19). Hmm..., that sounds familiar, doesn't it? In Exodus, God asked Moses to return to Egypt. In the New Testament, an angel of God asked someone in a dream that he should take his family and go to Egypt (Mathew 2:13-15). After a while, an angel of the Lord appears to the same man in another dream and is told to take his family back to their own country because those who sought to kill the young child were dead (Mathew 2:19-20). Who did the angel of God appear to? Who was the young child they were trying to kill? Who was the one that wanted to kill the young child?
   a. Joseph
   b. Jesus
   c. Herod

3, God had given Moses several signs for the Children of Israel, yet Moses still had another excuse for God. What was it?
   a. I cannot see very well.
   b. I cannot read very well.

c. I am not a good speaker.

d. I am a cripple.

4. Moses confessed to God that he was slow of speech and tongue (not a good speaker). God told him He was the one that made the mute, the deaf, the seeing, the blind and that he should go because He would be with _____.

a. His brain and show him what he shall think about

b. His legs and direct him where he shall go

c. His hands and show him what he shall hold

d. His mouth and teach him what to say

5. God had told Moses He would be with his mouth and teach him what to say, but Moses asked God to please send someone else. God was not happy with Moses, and He told him that somebody who was also a Levite that could speak was coming to meet him. The person would be happy in his heart when he sees Moses. Who was that person?

a. His uncle, Laban

b. His brother, Aaron

c. His brother, Shand

d. His sister, Miriam

6. God told Moses his brother, Aaron, was coming to meet him. Moses would speak to Aaron and put words in his mouth. God also said He would be with their mouths, teach Moses what to do, and Aaron would be Moses' speaker to the people. Again, He told Moses that Aaron would be a mouth to him, and Moses shall be like something to Aaron. What did God say Moses would be like to Aaron?

a. As god

b. A prophet

c. A leader

d. A director

7. Up till now, How many times had Moses resisted (given excuses why he couldn't do what God was asking him) the Lord before he finally gave in?

a. Three times

b. Four times

c. Five times

d. Six times

8. Finally, Moses agreed with God. He went back home to meet Jethro, his father-in-law, then he asked him to let him return to his people in Egypt to see whether they were still alive. Before Moses left Midian, God told him to return to Egypt because something had happened to the men that wanted to kill him. What happened to those men?
a. They had moved from Egypt.
b. They had lost their authority.
c. They were dead.
d. They were blind and could see him anymore.

9. When Moses went to Egypt, he went with _____?
a. His wife and father-in-law
b. His wife and two sons
c. His wife, two sons, and his father-in-law
d. His wife, two sons, father-in-law, and some of his sister-in-laws

10. Moses went back to Egypt with his wife and two boys, putting them in a carriage. He used a horse to transport his family. Is that true or false?

The Rod!

Here we see Moses giving one excuse after another to God why he cannot bring the Children of Israel out of Egypt. God was running out of patience with Moses, too. When Moses finally agreed and went to Egypt, he only had a rod in His hand apart from his family. You know, that rod is the only thing Moses needed to defeat the entire army of Egypt. We also have our rod with us now—the Bible. That is the only thing we need to write in our hearts that we can use to defeat every form of enemy that might come our way. Do you have your Bible? Do you read it? Do you do according to what is written in it or give excuses like Moses? Funny, ha?

Quiz 9
Read Exodus 4:20-31; 5:1-23, 6:1-3.

1.The rod Moses had in his hand at the burning bush in Horeb that turned into a snake was known by a different name when Moses returned to Egypt. What is the rod's name?
   a. The rod of the snake
   b. The miracle rod
   c. The rod of God
   d. The rod of power

2. The Lord asked Moses to describe Israel to Pharaoh. How did He ask Moses to describe the Children of Israel?
   a. Israel is His son, His firstborn
   b. Israel is His People
   c. Israel is His blood
   d. Israel is His eyeball that He had to protect with jealousy

3. God asked Moses to tell Pharaoh that he should let His firstborn go and serve Him. If Pharaoh refused, God would kill his firstborn. Is that true or false?

4. Moses and his family started their journey to Egypt, but they could not make it in a single day, so they camped. At their encampment, the Lord wanted to kill Moses, but Zipporah _____.
   a. Used a stone to hit Moses on his forehead
   b. Anointed Moses, so the Lord would not kill him.
   c. Hid her two sons.
   d. Took a sharp stone and cut off the foreskin of her son and cast it at Moses' feet.

5. The Lord wanted to kill Moses? What? Yes, He wanted to. Why?

6. In Egypt, the Lord told Aaron to go into the wilderness and meet Moses. Then he met him on the mountain of God. Moses told Aaron all the signs the Lord had asked him to perform. When they arrived at Goshen, they gathered the elders of the Children of Israel together, and Moses did _ _ _ _ _ _.
    a. The miracle of putting his hand under his armpit to turn it to snow and put it back to turn normal again
    b. The sign of the rod, which transforms into a snake
    c. The sign of the water turning into blood
    d. All the signs the Lord had shown him.

7. Moses showed the elders of the Children of Israel the signs the Lord had asked him to show to them. When Moses showed them the signs, they _ _ _ _ _ _.
    a. Said they wanted to think about it
    b. Asked him to change the blood water back to water
    c. Believed, bowed their heads, and worshipped
    d. Were surprised that God still remembered them

8. Moses and Aaron went to meet Pharoah and told him that the God of the Hebrews had said he should let His people go. Pharoah laughed and asked, "Who is the God of the Hebrews, that I should obey Him?" (Exodus 5:2). He did not know Him or His voice, so he would not obey Him. Then the King of Egypt said Moses and Aaron were stopping the people from doing their jobs. He commanded the taskmasters and their officers to stop giving the Israelites an ingredient used to make bricks. What was it he stopped the officers from giving to the Israelites?
    a. Stones
    b. Tiles
    c. Straw
    d. Bows

9. Pharaoh asked the officers not to give the people straw to make bricks, but the people were to make as many bricks as before. That increased the suffering of the Children of Israel, and the officers beat them, too. The officers of Israel went to complain to Pharoah, and he told them _____.

a. You are idle! That is why you have asked me to release you so you can offer your sacrifice to the Lord.

b. You hired Moses from the wilderness and asked him to tell me to let you go.

c. You are not working hard enough.

d. You are too lazy, and I want you to work harder to complete your tasks.

10. When the officers of Israel were coming from Pharaoh, they met Moses and Aaron. They said to them, "The Lord should look on you and judge you because you have made Pharoah to put the sword in the hand of the Egyptians to kill us." Moses went and talked to the Lord, who told him He appeared to Abraham, Isaac, and Jacob as one name. What is the name of God the three patriarchs knew?

a. God Almighty

b. Jehovah

c. God the Provider

d. Ancient of Days

The Word of God Sets Free!

Here, Moses and Aaron met with the elders of Israel. He did all the signs in their presence, and they believed, but when persecution from Pharaoh and his people arose, they called God to judge Moses and Aaron. The Word of God brings freedom to our lives, and the Devil does not want us to hear it. Just like the Israelites, Moses brought the Word of God to them so they would be free from their bondage, but when problems arose because of it, they deserted Moses and Aaron. Sometimes when you decide to stand for God, because His Word had set you free, you will have opposition from friends, classmates, families, etc. Will you be able to maintain your stand about what God had done and told you, or you will be like the Israelite's multitude?

You know, sometimes, our parents make decisions that are hard for us because they want our lives to be better for us, but some of those decisions don't always look good for us at the time they made them—moving to a new environment, changing schools, etc. What do you do in such a situation? Do you desert your parents, complain about how you moved away from your friends and school, or do you stay with them and encourage them even when it is hard for you? What do you do?

Circle the signs God gave Moses to show Israelites' elders in Egypt

Quiz 10
Read Exodus 6:3-30; 7:1-12.

1. God did not show the patriarchs (Abraham, Isaac, and Jacob) one of His names. What was the name of God that the three patriarchs did not know?
   a. Lord
   b. Jehovah
   c. The deliverer
   d. Savior

2. Aaron, brother of Moses, had five sons. Is that true or false?

3. What are the names of Aaron's sons?
   a. Abinadab, Abihu, Eleazar, and Ithamar
   b. Nadab, Abihu, Eleazer, and Ithamar
   c. Ephraim, Nadab, Abihu, and Ithamar
   d. Lamach, Abihu, Eleazer, and Ithamar

4. Eleazer, Aaron's son, had one son that was mentioned. What is the name of that son?
   a. Ephraim
   b. Lamach
   c. Phinehas
   d. Abinadab

5. In Egypt, God told Moses to go and speak to Pharoah. Moses told the Lord he is of the uncircumcised lip, so how can he talk to Pharoah? God informed Moses that He had made him like something to Pharaoh. What did God make Moses like to Pharaoh?
   a. As god
   b. A tormentor
   c. A thorn in his side

d. An adversary

6. God made Moses like a god to Pharaoh, and He made Aaron something to Moses. What did God make Aaron be for Moses?
   a. A speaker
   b. An interpreter
   c. A prophet
   d. A staff carrier

7. How old was Moses at this time?
   a. He was seventy-eight years old.
   b. He was eighty years old.
   c. He was eighty-five years old.
   d. He was eighty-seven years old.

8. At this time, Moses was eighty years old and Aaron was eighty-nine years old. Is that true or false?

9. Moses and Aaron appeared before Pharaoh, and he asked them to show him a miracle. Aaron cast his rod down, and the rod turned into a serpent. Yeah! Pharaoh called his sorcerers to cast theirs down, and they turned into a serpent, too. Ops! Aaron's rod did something to the sorcerers' rod. What did it do to them?
   a. Aaron's rod beat up the magicians'.
   b. Aaron's rod flogged the magicians' with its tail.
   c. Aaron's rod swallowed up the magicians' snake.
   d. Aaron's rod broke, and the magicians all died.

10. Because Pharaoh hardened his heart, God sent how many plagues to Egypt?
   a. Eight
   b. Nine
   c. Ten
   d. Eleven

Some Info!

Aaron is three years older than Moses. That means Aaron was born before Pharaoh started his decree of throwing every male boy in the river. Aaron had four sons. Two of Aaron's sons will be remembered for their wrong actions in the third series of this book—Leviticus (watch out for that). His third son, Eleazer, will become a very prominent person in Israel. Eleazer has a son named Phinehas. Phinehas is going to do something that pleased God in a time to come and God will give him His covenant of peace forever (You will discover all this in Leviticus and Numbers of this series. I can't wait to see and hear how those will unfold!)

You have worked so hard. Please take a moment and rest. Meditate on some things you have read or heard. Maybe you should ask your parents some questions and clarify things a little. Whoa! Are you excited? I am! Okay. See you on the next quiz!

Quiz 11
Read Exodus 714-25; 8:1-13.

1.God hardened Pharaoh's heart (Genesis 7:13; 9:12; 10:1; 20:27; 11:10; and 14:8). Is it unjust of God to harden Pharaoh's heart and not give him a chance to repent? What do you think about this?

2. When Pharoah saw the rod miracle, his heart grew hard, and he did not let the Children of Israel leave. Then, God told Moses to place the first plague on Egypt. What was the first plague, anyway?
a. Flies everywhere
b. Water becomes blood
c. Frogs
d. Darkness

3. Aaron had to do something in the presence of Pharaoh in the morning for the water to turn into blood. What did he do?
a. Moses stretched his rod over the waters of Egypt, the streams, rivers, ponds, and pools of water.
b. Aaron stretched the rod of God over the waters of Egypt, the streams, rivers, ponds, and pools of water.
c. Moses stretched his rod over the rivers, streams, and ponds.
d. Aaron stretched the rod of God over the rivers, streams, and ponds.

4. Moses and Aaron turned the waters of Egypt into blood in the presence of Pharaoh, who then called his magicians to do the same. Pharaoh's heart did not change, and he would not let the

Children of Israel leave Egypt. The bloody water stayed in Egypt for how many days?
a. Six days
b. Seven days
c. Eighty days
d. Nine days

5. The fishes in the rivers died when the water turned to blood. The people could not drink the water because it stank, but God was merciful to them. He made provision for them to get water for drinking. How did the people get their drinking water?
a. They dug all around the river to get water to drink.
b. They boiled the water and sieved it.
c. They added chemicals to the water to make it clean.
d. They left the fetched water under the sun so that it could take away the color and smell.

6. The Lord sent the second plague because Pharaoh refused to let the Children of Israel depart. What was the second plague?
a. Frogs
b. Flies
c. Death of animals
d. Locus

7. The frogs came from the rivers, ponds, and streams. Is that true or false?

8. When the pandemic of frogs came upon Egypt, Pharaoh called his magicians to do the same and brought more frogs onto the land of Egypt. Frogs upon frogs, "ribbit, ribbit" everywhere! Pharaoh summoned Moses and asked him to pray to the Lord that He might take away the plague. Moses asked Pharaoh, "When do you want the plague to be taken away?" Pharaoh said _____?
a. Now
b. Tomorrow
c. Day after tomorrow
d. In four days' time

9. Moses told Pharaoh that the frogs would leave their houses but stay in the forest, desert, fields, and river. Is that true or false?

10. Pharaoh asked Moses to pray to the Lord to take away the frogs. Moses cried to the Lord; God answered his prayer and took away the frogs. How did it happen?

a. The frogs jumped back into the rivers.
b. The frogs disappeared.
c. The frogs died.
d. The frogs evaporated.

First Two Plagues!

God hits Egypt with the first two plagues. These two plagues, after Moses and Aaron did their plagues, Pharaoh asked his magicians to perform them, and they counterfeited the plagues. Magicians didn't start counterfeiting stuff today, you know. They have been doing it even in the Bible days. I wonder if they will copy the next plague! What do you think?

Quiz 12
Read Exodus 8:14-24.

1.The people did something to the dead frogs. What did they do to them?
    a. They burned them.
    b. They buried them.
    c. They threw them into the river.
    d. They gathered them together in heaps.

2. What happened to the land when the people gathered the dead frogs in heaps?
    a. It stank.
    b. It vibrated.
    c. It smoked.
    d. It turned green for a while.

3. Pharaoh was relieved of the frogs, then thanked God and Moses. Is that true or false?

4. God took away the second plague, which was frogs everywhere, but Pharaoh hardened his heart again. Then God sent the third plague, which was _____ in Egypt.
    a. Flies
    b. Lice
    c. Darkness
    d. Death of animals

5. Lice came because God asked Moses to tell Aaron to _____.
    a. Stretch the rod into the river.
    b. Stretch the rod towards the desert.
    c. Stretch out his rod and strike the land's dust.
    d. Stretch out the rod towards Heaven.

6. Aaron stretched out his rod and struck the land's dust, and all the dust became lice. Pharaoh instructed his magicians to do the same. What could his magicians do?

a. They brought out more lice.

b. They brought out dust to replace the ones that turned into lice.

c. They brought out lice nets to cover the people from the lice.

d. They could not bring out lice.

7. The magicians could not bring out lice like they could turn water into blood and produce frogs. Ouch! Who suffered from the lice?

a. Only the men and women. The kids were excluded because they were innocent.

b. The lice were on the men and Pharaoh's household only.

c. The lice were on every human being.

d. The lice were on both human beings and beasts.

8. When the magicians could not bring forth lice, they said what to Pharoah?

a. They said, "Leave the Israelites alone."

b. They said, "The Lord is God!"

c. They said, "This is the finger of God."

d. They said, "We are doomed!"

9. Our merciful God took away the lice's plague, hurrah! Pharaoh again hardened his heart, so God brought them the fourth plague. What was the fourth plague God brought?

a. Flies

b. Mouse

c. Darkness

d. Death of animals

Finger of God!

Wow! What was your guess about the third plague? Did you say the magicians will copy it or not? Well, they could not. Praise God! Hmm, to make things more interesting, they recognized the supremacy of God, for they said, "This is the finger of God" (Exodus 8:19). Do you always recognize the finger of God (hand of God) in your life every day? Try looking for it. I'm sure you will find it.

Quiz 13
Read Exodus 8:20-32; 9:1-7.

Pharaoh hardened his heart and did not let the Children of Israel go. God asked Moses to meet Pharaoh in the morning, as he came out of the water and charged him to let His people go or He would bring swarms of flies upon the land. What will God do differently with this plague?

a. He will differentiate between the Egyptians' houses so that only the rich will receive the plague of flies.

b. He will differentiate between the Egyptians' houses so that only the Pharaoh's household will receive the plague of flies.

c. He will put a difference between the Egyptians' houses so that only those in support of Pharaoh and his evil deeds will receive the plague of flies.

d. Only the Egyptians will receive the plague of the flies, but Goshen, where the Israelites lived, will not have swarms of flies.

2. God sent the plague of flies on the Egyptians, and they were not in Goshen where the Israelites lived because the Lord wanted Pharoah to know something. What did He want Pharoah to know?

a. He is the Lord amidst the land.

b. He is a miracle worker.

c. He is in control of everything that is happening.

d. He is super.

3. The Lord sent a thick swarm of flies into Egypt, and there were none in Goshen. Pharaoh sent for Moses and asked him to _____.

a. Go and sacrifice to his God in the wilderness.

b. Go and sacrifice to his God in the land.

c. Go and sacrifice to his God in their temple.

d. Go and sacrifice to his God at night.

4. Pharaoh had asked Moses to go and sacrifice to the Lord in Egypt, but Moses told him it would not be good for them to sacrifice in Egypt because _____.

a. The Egyptians would hate their sacrifices (for they would complain to God about the Egyptians) and want to stone them.

b. They would tell the Lord how horrible the Egyptians had been to them, crying, and that will bring a fight.

c. They would tell the Lord how they wanted the Egyptians to die and call for war.

e. They cannot sacrifice to their God in a foreign land.

5. Moses told the Pharaoh they could not sacrifice to the Lord in Egypt because they would put the abomination of Egypt towards them before Him. If the Egyptians saw that, they would stone them. Because of that reason, Moses told Pharaoh that _____.

a. They would go on a two-day journey into the wilderness and sacrifice to the Lord their God.

b. They would go on a three-day journey into the wilderness and sacrifice to the Lord their God.

c. They would go on a four-day journey into the wilderness and sacrifice to the Lord their God.

d. They would go on a five-day journey into the wilderness and sacrifice to the Lord their God.

6. Moses told Pharaoh they would go on a three-day journey into the wilderness and sacrifice to the Lord their God. Pharoah agreed and asked Moses to do him a favor. What did he ask for?

a. Please do not go out of the land of Egypt and intercede for me.

b. Do not go far away and intercede for me.

c. Go a little out of the land of Goshen and intercede for me.

d. I was hoping you would not go far away and do not intercede for me.

7. Moses prayed to God to take away the swarms of flies. God answered Moses' prayer and took the plague of flies away. What did Pharaoh do?

a. He hardened his heart and did not keep his promise of letting them go away to sacrifice and intercede for him.

b. He let the Children of Israel go away to sacrifice but sent soldiers along with them.

c. He told Moses he did not agree to let them leave.

d. He asked Moses to leave his sight.

8. The Lord sent the fifth plague because Pharaoh refused to let the Children of Israel go as he had promised. The fifth plague was darkness and rain. Is that true or false?

9. Pharaoh refused to keep to his promise by letting the Hebrews leave, so the Lord sent the death of the livestock plague, but the Lord did something. What did He do?

a. He put a difference between the clean and unclean animals, so only the unclean ones died.

b. He sent the plague to the livestock of Pharaoh, his magicians, and wise men alone.

c. He sent the plague to only the servants' livestock

d. He put a difference between the livestock of the Egyptians and that of the Israelites because it was only the Egyptians' livestock that died.

10. The Lord sent the plague on the Egyptians' livestock the next day, as He had said. When Pharaoh saw that their livestock was dead, he

_____.

a. Buried them

b. Invoked the god of death to appear in Goshen

c. Sent to know if the livestock of the Children of Israel had died

d. Mourned for his livestock

Faithful God!

Well, God is faithful. The Israelites live in Egypt, but the plague did not come near their dwelling because He put a difference between His people and the ungodly. Do you know Psalm 91 is related to what happened in Egypt? Take a break, and read it. You will know how God is always protecting His people from danger. Come on, go ahead and read it. I will see you on the next quiz.

Quiz 14
Read Exodus 9:8-27.

1.God had placed the plague of livestock's death on the Land of the Egyptians, and Pharaoh hardened his heart because he did not let the Hebrews leave. God sent the next (sixth) plague, which was _____.
   a. Darkness
   b. Flood
   c. Rotten food
   d. Boils that break out in sores

2. Pharaoh refused to let the Hebrews leave. Then God asked Moses to trigger the plague of boils. What did God ask Moses to do that brought this plague?
   a. He asked him to take dust from the sea and throw it to the heavens in the presence of Pharaoh.
   b. He asked him to take dirt from under a tree and throw it towards the desert in the presence of Pharaoh.
   c. He asked him to take dry leaves, squeeze them together, and spread them around Pharaoh.
   d. He asked him to take a handful of ashes from a furnace and scatter it toward the heavens in the sight of Pharaoh.

3. God asked Moses to take a handful of ashes from a furnace and scatter it toward the heavens in the sight of Pharaoh. When Moses did that, the ashes became fine dust and turn to boils. Is that true or false?

4. The plague of boils was upon _____.
   a. Men only
   b. Men and women only
   c. Man and beast
   d. Wealthy households only

5. Again, Pharaoh did not let the Children of Israel leave, so God sent the seventh plague. What was this plague?

a. Flood

b. Darkness

c. Rotten food

d. Hail

6. God said Pharaoh was raised for a reason. What was the reason?

a. That He might show His power in him and His name may be declared in all the earth

b. That he may be a stubborn goat

c. That he may use him to serve as an example to all people in the world

d. That he may know the power of the Most High God

7. God, through Moses, told Pharaoh that He would send hail to Egypt that would kill the livestock. For that reason, he should send and gather the livestock from the fields, for it would hail on _____ that was not brought in from the fields?

a. Every animal

b. Every horse and camel

c. Every animal that has four legs

d. Every man, beast, and herb

8. God was merciful to the people and asked them to remove their livestock and servants (humans) from the field so they would not die. Some people did not remove theirs, but the magicians, wise men, and Pharaoh's loyalist removed their servants and animals. Is that true or false?

9. God asked Moses to do something to initiate the hail. What did He ask Moses to do?

a. Stretch out his hand toward the rivers.

b. Stretch out his hand toward the east.

c. Stretch out his hand toward Canaan.

d. Stretch out his hand toward Heaven.

10. The Lord sent the plague of hail to Egypt onto every man, beast, and herb. The trees broke in the fields, but it did not hail in Goshen. Pharaoh sent for Moses and said he had _____.

a. Deceived Moses and Aaron several times, but not this time

b. Misunderstood Moses and Israel again

c. Lied to Moses and his God again

d. Sinned this time. The Lord is righteous, and my people and I are wicked.

Merciful God!

God is a God of mercy. Here, we saw Him giving the people that were punishing His children the opportunity to gather their servants and livestock from the farm before He releases hail on the land. Well, some people obeyed the voice of God, and others didn't. Those who listened were saved from the disaster while those who did not were destroyed. Making the right choice is very important in this world. Many people have suffered, some are suffering, and others will still suffer because of their bad choices. Have you ever made any decision that landed you in trouble? What did you do? What did you do about it? Was it fun to have suffered because of the wrong choices you made? I need you to think about what you did and what you will do differently to avoid a similar situation. I want you to think about some actions you can take to ensure that you always make the best decision.

Quiz 15
Read Exodus 9:28-35; 10:1-17.

Pharaoh asked Moses to pray to God that he might stop the thundering and hail. He promised to let Israel go. Moses told Pharaoh he would _ _ _ _ _ _ as soon as he left the city, the thunder would cease.
 a. Pray to the Lord.
 b. Spread out his hands to the Lord.
 c. Use his rod to hit the muddy water.
 d. Use his rod to draw a line towards the river.

2. When the Lord sent the hail, three crops were mentioned. What were the names of the three crops?
 a. The flax, barley, and wheat
 b. The flax, wheat, and olive
 c. The wheat, flax, and corn
 d. The wheat, barley, and corn

3. The hail did not strike the wheat because it was a late crop. Is that true or false?

4. Moses spread out his hands to the Lord, and He stopped the hail and thundering. Pharaoh's heart hardened once more, and he refused to let Israel depart. The Lord told Moses that He wanted these signs to be spoken to?
 a. The hearing of their daughters who married outside the tribe of Israel
 b. The hearing of their sons and son's sons
 c. The hearing of the non-Jews
 d. The hearing of the Egyptians

5. Pharaoh still did not let the Children of Israel leave Egypt, so Moses went back to meet him at the command of the Lord, telling him of the eighth plague. What then is this plague?
a. Drought
b. Flood
c. Darkness
d. Locusts

6. Moses told Pharaoh of the coming locust plague that would destroy what was left of Egypt's fields. This time, Pharaoh said nothing to Moses, but his servants said he should let the Israelites go because the man, Moses, had been a snare to them. Then Pharoah sent for Moses and Aaron. He asked them who would go to offer sacrifices to the Lord. Moses told him they would go with all they had. Pharaoh warned Moses that the Lord had better be with them when he freed them and the infants. He warned them to exercise caution because evil lies in wait for them. Then Pharaoh said to Moses that only some people could go and serve the Lord. The rest would remain in Egypt. Who was allowed to go serve the Lord, according to Pharaoh?
a. The men
b. The women
c. The young adults
d. The children

7. Pharaoh instructed Moses that only the men could go and serve the Lord, but Moses said no, they would all go with their flocks. Pharaoh's servants did something to Moses and Aaron. What did they do to them?
a. They walked them out with their soldiers.
b. They drove them out of Pharaoh's presence.
c. They made them a feast.
d. They flogged them.

8. When Moses left Pharoah, the Lord asked him to do something so that the locusts might flood into Egypt. What did God ask Moses to do?
a. Stretch out his hand (rod) over the land of Egypt.
b. Stretch out his hand (rod) to the east.
c. Stretch out his hand (rod) towards Heaven.
d. Stretch out his hand (rod) north.

9. Moses obeyed God, stretched out his rod over Egypt, and the Lord brought south and north wind over the land all that day and night. Is that true or false?

10. At dawn, the east wind brought locusts into the land, and they devoured the leftover trees, herbs, fruits, and plants of the field, throughout Egypt and its territories. Pharaoh called Moses and Aaron in a hurry and said, _____.

a. He had brought the Israelites too much trouble. They should petition the Lord for them this last time.

b. He had sinned against the Lord, their God, and them. They should forgive his sin this time and entreat the Lord their God to take this death away from him only this time.

c. He had sinned against their God. They should entreat Him to spare some plants for his people and himself. Then he will let the Israelites go this time.

d. He was genuinely sorry for not letting them go. They should please pray to their God so He might stop this disaster.

God is Interested in You!

Here we saw the plague of hail and locusts on the entire land of Egypt, except for Goshen, where the Children of Israel lived. Pharaoh and his people were feeling the effect of what God was doing, so his people advised him to let the Children of Israel leave. When they summoned Moses and Aaron, Pharoah said only the men could go and worship the Lord God. Well, God is interested in every single soul—slave, elderly, rich, poor, and even children. He is so concerned about His children. Jesus showed us how much God loved kids in the story below:

In Mark 10:13-16, some women wanted Jesus to bless their children. These women and their little ones pushed their way to the front of the crowd, but the disciples would have none of it. They began chasing away the women and their kids. When Jesus saw this, He stopped them. He asked the women to bring their children to Him. He took the children up in His arms and blessed all of them. The mothers and children were thrilled. Jesus, the Son of God, had blessed them. Jesus wants all children to know that He loves them and wants to bless them. Receive His blessings today!

Do you know Jesus wants you to be with Him all the time?

Do you know He knows your name and the number of the hair on your head?

How are you doing so far? Come on, give yourself a pat on the back. You are doing great, really. Don't worry if you missed some, but you don't have to give up either. Read the Bible passage and answer the quizzes. Before you know it, you will improve very well. Everyone started from where you are now, you know. The more you read and listen, the more you will know about it. Good job!

Quiz 16
Read Exodus 10:18-29.

Pharaoh asked Moses and Aaron to forgive his sin only this last time so they could entreat the Lord their God to take away the locusts from the land. Moses left Pharaoh's presence and entreated the Lord; then He sent _ _ _ _ _ _ to take away the locusts.
    a. A strong east wind
    b. A strong south wind
    c. A strong north wind
    d. A strong west wind

2. The strong west wind the Lord sent blew the locusts to the desert, forest, ponds, and pools. Is that true or false?

3. When Pharaoh realized the locusts were all gone, he did not let the Children of Israel go, for the Lord had hardened his heart. Therefore, the Lord sent the plague of _ _ _ _ _ _ _ on Egypt.
    a. Flood
    b. Rotten food
    c. Darkness
    d. Drought

4. When Pharaoh refused to let the Hebrews depart, the Lord commanded Moses to take action, which caused darkness that could be felt to descend upon Egypt. What did the Lord ask Moses to do?
    a. Stretch his rod towards the four corners of the earth.
    b. Stretch his hand toward Heaven.
    c. Stretch his hand to the east, where the sun rises.
    d. Stretch his hand to the west, where the sunset.

5. The darkness lasted for _ _ _ _ _ _ _ in Egypt.
    a. Two days

b. Three days
c. Four days
d. Five days

6. The darkness was felt throughout the land of Egypt, except for Goshen. The Egyptians could not leave their homes, and neither were they able to see one another. Then Pharaoh sent for Moses and asked him to go and serve the Lord, but he gave Moses a condition. What was the condition he gave to Moses?
a. He asked Moses to let their little ones stay behind.
b. He asked Moses to let their wives stay behind.
c. He asked Moses to let their young adult stay behind.
d. He asked Moses to let their flocks and herds stay behind.

7. Moses told Pharaoh that they must go with everything they had, even their flock because they would use some animals to sacrifice to the Lord their God. He said they didn't know which animals they would use for the offering until they arrived. Then Pharaoh was mad and asked Moses to _____.
a. Go away from him and be careful not to see his face again because the day he does, he will die.
b. Get away from him and hang himself.
c. Get away from him. He doesn't want to see him again in his palace.
d. Go away, for his request cannot be granted because he was so rude and heartless.

8. What was Moses' reply to Pharaoh when he said he shouldn't see his face again?
a. You have no such power because I will be here tomorrow.
b. You cannot kill me; only God can.
c. I will come here until you let God's people go.
d. Well-spoken, I will never see your face again.

9. The Passover lamb is symbolic of our Lord Jesus Christ (1 Corinthians 5:7). It had to be without blemish, which symbolized

Jesus being without sin (Hebrew 4:15). In the same way, the Is-raelites had to eat this lamb, so we must eat of Christ's body (John 6:53-58). And when the lamb's blood was applied to the doorposts of their homes, the death angel passed over them, doing them no harm. Likewise, when we make Jesus our personal Savior, His blood is applied to our lives, and Satan/hell has to pass over us. We have passed from death unto life (John 5:24). Praise God! During Passover, a family used one lamb. Smaller families could share a lamb because they were all saved together. What is the difference between the Passover lamb and Jesus concerning salvation?

10. Pharaoh had asked Moses to leave his presence and not see his face again; otherwise, he would die. Moses gladly left and waited for what God would say next. The Lord told Moses He would bring one more plague on Egypt, and then Pharaoh would drive them away. The Lord asked Moses to prepare the Israelites for the last and tenth plague. What was that plague, anyway?
a. Rotten food
b. Flood
c. Death of the Egyptian's firstborn
d. Confusion

Pray for Our Government!

We have seen Pharaoh making promises he will not keep. There had been three solid days of total darkness. No one could move. I can imagine people opening their eyes so wide to see something to no avail. You know it is normal to open your eyes wide to see better when the place is dark, right? Has that happened to you before? Oh, what about the kids? I feel sorry for them because they cried and cried. They wanted to see their mom, but nay! When they were hungry, they couldn't eat because their moms couldn't see to make food. It was a compulsory fast. Hmm, do you know what hunger can do to someone? It can make you do silly things. Oh, oh, oh, I remember Esau. He sold his birthright because of hunger, remember?

Take a moment to think. Why was everyone suffering? What was your answer? You got it—bad Government. If only Pharaoh had listened to God, the suffering will not have happened to the entire country. It is not different for us today. There are lots of countries suffering from poverty, war, etc, because of corrupt governments. Therefore, we should pray for them to always make the right decision. Do you know why? If they make a wrong decision, it will not affect them alone because their evil decisions will rub on everybody. Here comes the question: have you ever prayed for your government? The government doesn't have to be the president, prime minister, king, or queen alone. Your parents are your government, too. Even the school authority, local government, etc. please pray for them. The Bible even asked us to pray for kings and all those in authority (1 Timothy 2:1-3). From now on, whenever you are praying, please pray for them so we can live a better life.

Quiz 17
Read Exodus 11:1-10; 12:1-5.

1.God warned Moses that after the final plague, Pharaoh would expel the Israelites, therefore Moses was tasked with telling the populace to ask their neighbors for gifts of silver and gold. Then the Lord gave the Israelites _____before the Egyptians.
   a. Peace
   b. Happiness
   c. Joy
   d. Favor

2. Moses announced to the people that the Lord said, about midday, He would go into the midst of Egypt, and their firstborn would die, even the firstborn of Pharaoh. Is that true or false?

3. The Lord said He would go into the midst of Egypt at midnight, and all their firstborns would die. The firstborn's death involved _____.
   a. Only the firstborn of Pharaoh
   b. The firstborn of all the human beings in Egypt
   c. The firstborn of both humans and animals
   d. The firstborn of Pharaoh and all those that supported him in his evil deeds

4. In Egypt, Moses was mighty. In whose eyes was he great?
   a. In the sight of the servants
   b. In the eyes of the servants and the magicians
   c. In the view of the magicians and Pharoah
   b. In the sight of Pharaoh's servants and the people

5. God said to Moses that this month should be the beginning of the year for them. Which month was He referring to?
   a. The month of Abib

b. The month of Saturs

c. The month of Freedom

d. The month of Release

6. When God was talking to Moses, He gave him the day on which he was to carry out the instructions. What was the day?

a. On the eighth of the month

b. On the ninth of the month

c. On the tenth of the month

d. On the eleventh of the month

7. God said to Moses that each family should take a particular animal. What is the animal's name each family should use?

a. A ram

b. A lamb

c. A sheep

d. A dove

8. God gave a condition that requires two or three families to use a lamb together. What is that condition?

a. If the family is unclean, it should look for a clean family to share a lamb with.

b. Two or three unclean families should share a lamb.

c. A poor and wealthy family should share a lamb.

d. If a family is too small, that family and his neighbor should take a lamb according to each man's needs.

9. The Lord said that the lamb each family (families) will use should be _____.

a. Without blemish

b. Without one eye

c. Without talking

d. Without struggling

10. The lamb each family will use had to be female in the first year. Is that true or false?

The Passover!

This is where the Lord instituted the Passover. The Passover is the eating of roasted lamb with bitter herbs and unleavened bread. It is a feat and is sometimes called the Feast of Unleavened

Bread. It is celebrated once a year. Oh, I hope I'm not giving away some answers. I'd better stop here.

How many did you score this time? Did you read the Bible passage before answering or did you answer before reading? Always try to double-check your answers so you don't keep the wrong one in your heart. Wow! You are doing great! Keep up the momentum! I will see you on the other quiz.

Quiz 18
Read Exodus 12:5-12.

1.The people may take the lamb from _____.
   a. Sheep of dove
   b. Sheep or cow
   c. Goat or dove
   d. Sheep or goat

2. When the people have taken the lamb, they shall keep it until another date of the same month. What is that date?
   a. The twelve-day
   b. The thirteenth-day
   c. The fourteenth-day
   d. The fifteenth-day

3. On the fourteenth day of the month, Israel's congregation shall kill the lamb _____.
   a. In the morning
   b. At noon
   c. In the evening
   d. At midnight

4. When the lamb was killed, the people were to place its blood _____.
   a. On the back and front doors of their houses
   b. On the lintel and at the front door of their houses
   c. On their houses' two doorposts and lintel
   d. On the lintel and the foot match of their houses

5. The Israelites were to eat the flesh on that night. God told them how they should cook the lamb. How was it cooked?
   a. It was cooked on the stovetop
   b. It was cooked in the oven

c. It was baked

d. It was roasted

6. The Children of Israel were to roast the lamb and eat the flesh with unleavened bread and sweet herbs. Is that true or false?

7. The Hebrews shall not eat the lamb raw nor boil it with water, but they shall roast it with its legs, entrails, and head. They will allow none of it to remain until morning, and they shall _____ the leftovers.

a. Bake

b. Bury

c. Smoke

d. Burn

8. The Children of Israel shall eat the lamb with a belt on their waist, sandals on their feet, and staff in their hands. Is that true or false?

9. This lamb, unleavened bread, and bitter herb eating are called _____.

a. The Lord's Passover

b. The Lord's Haste Eating

c. The Lord's feast of the Tabernacle

d. The Lord's Good Deeds

10. The Israelites shall eat the Lord's Passover _____.

a. In haste

b. Slowly

c. Joyfully

d. Happily

Rules for the Lord's Passover!

The Lord's Passover is still unfolding. Both sheep and goats are referred to as lambs. They selected the lamb on the tenth of the month of Abib. They have to keep it until the fourteenth day when they will kill it in the evening. The lamb must be a male and it must not have any blemish (defect). They will put some of its blood on the doorpost and lintel of their houses. They will eat the flesh (not bones). The cooking is only roasting. They must break none of its bones. There should be no leftovers. Every leftover they shall burn with fire. They were to eat it in haste (hurry) with their shoes on, belts on their waist, and staff in their hands. I think this is a faith move. God, through Moses, asked them to pack all they had. They even borrowed things from the Egyptians and were all dressed to leave in the morning while they were still in bondage. Pharaoh had not issued their freedom or go-and-worship-your-God decree, yet they were ready to roll. I am learning here that there are times we need to do things (take action) by faith against the odds. God told them they will leave, and they believed it. They did not wait to quote "seeing is believing" first. They believed without seeing and what they believed came to pass. How outstanding! Oh, that is why the Bible tells us in 2 Corinthians 5:7 to walk by faith and not by sight. Hmm..., will you try this out? When you pray about something, you believe God has answered you and thank Him for it.

Quiz 19
Read exodus 12:12-27.

1.On Passover night, the Lord will pass through the land of Egypt and strike all the firstborn, both man and beast. He will execute judgment 0n _____.
    a. Pharoah and his magicians
    b. Pharaoh and his firstborn
    c. The gods of Egypt
    d. The inhabitants of Egypt

2. God will turn His eyes off the Israelites when He sees the blood on the posts and lintels of their houses on the day He will strike the land of Egypt. Is that true or false?

3. The Lord said to the Hebrews that the Passover should be a memorial to them. They shall keep the Feast to the Lord throughout their generations, and they shall keep the feast by an everlasting ordinance. The Passover Feast shall last for _____.
    a. Five days
    b. Six days
    c. Seven days
    d. Eight days

4. When the Israelites keep the Feast of Passover, they shall remove _____ from their houses on the first day.
    a. Leaven
    b. Bread
    c. Oil
    d. Salt

5. Throughout the seven days of the Passover feast, anybody who eats leaven _____.
    a. Will be banished

b. Will be suspended for seven days
c. Will be cut off
d. Will be a slave to their neighbor

6. On the first day of the Passover Feast, there shall be a holy convocation, and on the seventh day, there shall be _____ to the Hebrews.
   a. A mourning
   b. A holy convocation
   c. A jubilee
   d. A wailing

7. On the fourteenth day of the first (Abib) month in the evening, they shall eat unleavened bread until the twenty-first day of the month in the evening. The rule of unleavened bread is given to _____.
   a. Only the Israelites
   b. Strangers or natives of the land
   c. Only the adult Israelites
   d. Only those that came from Egypt among the Israelites

8. The lamb they use for this feast is called the lamb of the unleavened, or the lamb of freedom. Is that true or false?

9. When Moses narrated what the Lord told him about the Passover to the elders, they _____.
   a. Yelled for joy
   b. Sang a praise song to the Lord their God
   c. Shook hands with Moses for being such a good leader
   d. Bowed their heads and worshiped

10. The Israelites applied the blood of the lamb on the doorpost of their houses and when the Angel of Death passed through the whole of Egypt; He passed over those houses. Hmm..., the Angel of Death saw the blood and passed over. He didn't bother

looking inside those houses. That means some Egyptians might have been inside the houses of the Israelites and would have been saved. I am thinking here. Why do you think God did not bother to look at the people inside the houses?

Circle the picture that was part of the Passover and X the one that wasn't.

Lamb without blemish (defect)

Pizza

Bitter Herbs

Hen

Doorposts

Popsicles

Unleavened Bread

Green Grapes

Quiz 20
Read Exodus 12:28-51; 13:1-10.

1. On the night of the Passover, the Lord moved throughout Egypt and struck all the firstborns, from the firstborn of Pharaoh, who sits on the throne, to the firstborn in their dungeon, their captives, and the firstborn of the animals. Then Pharaoh arose at night, called Moses and Aaron, telling them to arise and go from among them. This time, he said they should go with their children and their flocks and serve the Lord as they had said. He also said, _____.
   a. They should bless him, as well.
   b. They should serve him cake now, too.
   c. They should not come back to the land of Egypt.
   d. They should remember him.

2. When the Children of Israel left, they journeyed from Rameses to _____.
   a. Meribah
   b. Succoth
   c. Media
   d. The Red Sea

3. The Children of Israel moved from Rameses to Succoth. Several men were on foot. How many men were on foot?
   a. Four hundred thousand men
   b. Five hundred thousand men
   c. Six hundred thousand men
   d. Seven hundred thousand men

4. How can you work as a team with your parents to discover God's goodness?

5. A mixed multitude went up with the Children of Israel and much livestock. They also baked unleavened cakes of dough, which they brought from Egypt. The Bible gave the reason they baked unleavened cakes. What was the reason given?
a. They loved it.
b. They wanted to eat unleavened bread/cakes for seven days.
c. They forgot their leavenings.
d. They were driven out of Egypt and could not wait, nor did they prepare provisions for themselves.

6. How many years did the Children of Israel live without their permanent home?
a. Four hundred and twenty years
b. Four hundred and thirty years
c. Four hundred and forty years
d. Four hundred and fifty years

7. The Lord told Moses and Aaron that no foreigner should eat the Passover except one group of people. What is the group of people that can eat the Passover?
a. A sojourner
b. A hired personnel
c. Every man's servant that is bought with money
d. Every man's servant that is bought with money and is circumcised

8. God gave two rules concerning the Lamb of the Passover when it's being eaten. What were those two rules?
a. They shall break none of its bones and shall not eat it when it is cold.
b. They shall break none of its bones and shall take none of its flesh outside.

c. They shall not eat it in the daylight, and they shall wrap their heads when eating it.

d. They shall not eat it while sitting, and they shall eat it on the open field.

9. The Passover feast is also known as the Feast of the Unleavened Bread. Is that true or false?

10. The Lord said they should consecrate the firstborn of _____ to Him.
   a. Man
   b. Man, that is a male
   c. Both man and beast
   d. Both man and beast that is male

Death of Firstborn and Freedom!

Phew! Here, Pharaoh released the Children of Israel after the Angel of Death killed his firstborn, that of the Egyptians and the firstborn of animals. Remember, God sent the Angel of Death to execute judgment on the land for their disobedience and their gods. Pharaoh asked Moses to also bless him. Anyway, the Israelites are on their way to freedom from slavery now. What next?

How are you doing so far? Come on, give yourself a pat on the back. You are doing great, really. Don't worry if you missed some, but you don't have to give up either. Read the Bible passage and answer the quizzes. Before you know it, you will improve very well. Everyone started from where you are now, you know. The more you read and listen, the more you will know about it. Good job!

Number the plagues in the order they happened.

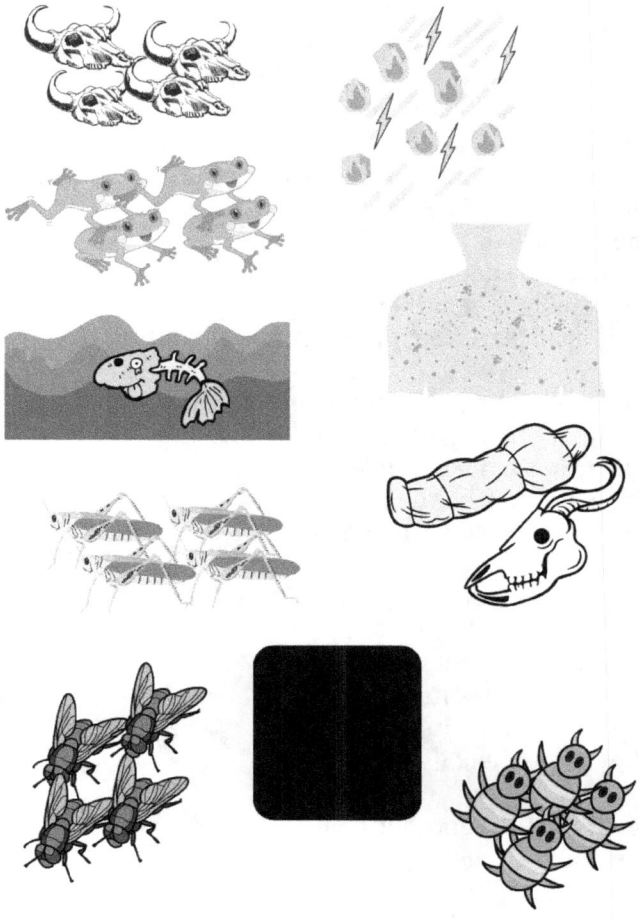

Quiz 21
Read Exodus 13:11-21.

1.Moses said they should consecrate the firstborn of both man and beast to the Lord, but he said something concerning the firstborn of man and donkey. What did he say?
   a. They shall always visit them.
   b. They shall redeem them with a dove.
   c. They shall redeem them with a lamb.
   d. They shall leave them to serve the Lord their God.

2. What will happen to an animal's firstborn males?
   a. The male shall be slaughtered before the Lord.
   b. The male shall be removed from among the herd.
   c. The male shall be the Lord's.
   d. The male shall be redeemed with a lamb.

3. God said the people should redeem the firstborn of a donkey with a lamb, but if they do not redeem it, _____.
   a. They shall break its legs.
   b. They shall break its neck.
   c. They shall break its tummy.
   d. They shall break its eye.

4. Egypt is called another name. What is that name?
   a. The house of the ungodly
   b. The house of bondage
   c. The house of evil
   d. The house of condemnation

5. Moses told the people if their sons should ask them why they are consecrating the firstborn of both man and beast to the Lord, they should tell them _____.
   a. The firstborns are always the Lord's forever.

b. When Pharaoh refused to let them go from Egypt, the Lord killed their firstborn of man and beast.

c. Their firstborn represents the firstborn of man and the beast of the evil people.

d. The firstborn is unique to the Lord.

6. When the Children of Israel left Egypt, the Lord did not lead them through the Philistines, which was nearer. Why?

a. The people might go back to Egypt if they saw war.

b. The people will decide to stay in the land of the Philistines.

c. The Lord did not want them to marry the Philistines.

d. The way of the Philistines was too rough.

7. When the Children of Israel were leaving, they took the bones of Joseph, who had placed the Israelites under a solemn oath to do so. Is that true or false?

8. When they journeyed from Succoth, they camped in _____.

a. Etham

b. Ai

c. Midei

d. Landall

9. The people journeyed from Succoth and camped at Etham, at _____.

a. The edge of the wilderness.

b. The edge of a huge rock

c. The edge of a stream.

d. The edge of the mountain cities

10. By day, the Lord went before them in a pillar of _____ to lead the way.

a. Cloud

b. Fire

c. Smoke

d. Lightning

Israelites Kept their Promise to Joseph!

The Israelites started their journey from Goshen and camped at Succoth. Goshen, where the Israelites lived in Egypt, is sometimes called Rameses. They camped in Etham which was near the wilderness.

When they started their journey, Moses took the bones of Joseph with him. Joseph was the son of Jacob. His brothers sold him into slavery in Egypt. He lived there for twenty-two years before he reunited with his family. Before he died, he prophesied to the Israelites that one day, God will visit and bring them out of Egypt into the land He had promised their fathers. When that happens, he made them swear an oath that they will carry his bones along with them (Genesis 50:22-26). So, when God freed them, they decide to carry his bones by keeping their promise to him.

Quiz 22
Read Exodus 13:21-22; 14:1-13.

1.By night, the Lord went before them in a pillar of smoke and lightning. Is that true or false?

2. The Lord went before them in a pillar of fire by night. Why?
a. To keep them warm
b. To cook their meal before they move in the morning
c. To give them light so they could travel day and night
d. To scare their enemies

3. Before the Israelites crossed the Red Sea, the Lord spoke to them, through Moses, that they should turn and camp at _____.
a. Medog
b. Sandel
c. Pi Hahiroth
d. Eden

4. Pi Hahiroth was between Migdol and _____.
a. The sea
b. The mountain
c. The valley of Ai
d. The desert

5. The Lord asked the people to camp at Pi Hahiroth, between Migdol and the sea. There was something opposite to this very place. What was it?
a. Baal Zephon
b. Mountain
c. Desert
d. The valley of Ai

6. Pharoah heard the Children of Israel had left, and he regretted ever letting them go, so he gathered his people and took some choice chariots. Each of these chariots had a captain. How many captains did he take?

    a. Four hundred
    b. Five hundred
    c. Six hundred
    d. Seven hundred

7. When the Children of Israel left Egypt, they went out smiling, shouting, and double-minded. Is that true or false?

8. Pharoah and his army overtook the Children of Israel at Pi Hahiroth before Baal Zephon. When the people saw the army of Pharoah marching behind them, they cried to the Lord and asked Moses a question. What did they ask Moses?

    a. Did you really think God is out here to help us?
    b. Why have you taken us out of Egypt?
    c. How many times do you have to provoke Pharoah?
    d. Did you bring us to die in the wilderness because there are no graves in Egypt?

9. Some Israelites were not willing to leave Egypt because of the third question they asked Moses. What was that question?

    a. Didn't we ask you to leave us in Egypt so we can serve Pharoah?
    b. Didn't we tell you we don't care whatever Pharoah does to us?
    c. Didn't we say we had lots of food to eat in Egypt?
    d. Didn't we say we cannot rule ourselves and that Pharoah can protect us?

10. The people were scared, and they questioned Moses and told him it would have been better for them to die in Egypt. When Moses heard all these questions, he said, _____.

    a. Stand still and see what the Lord will do to you.
    b. Stand still, for the Lord will drive Pharoah away from you today.
    c. Do not be afraid. Stand still and see the salvation of the Lord, which He will accomplish for you today.

d. Do not be afraid like the chicken. Remain calm and rejoice, for you will be exalted before the Egyptians today.

Do You Know God's Plan?

We talked about how the Children of Israel had faith when they were observing the Passover. They were all dressed, with their shoes on, belts on their waist, and staff in their hands as they eat the Passover in haste. At that time, Pharaoh had not allowed them to go, but they believed they would be leaving. In verse 8 of Exodus 14, we knew how they left Egypt with boldness-victory! The Egyptians didn't care about them, and why should they? They had their children, parents, aunts, uncles; you name it, to bury. Pharaoh was now behind them, and they were in front of the Red Sea.

Bringing Israel to camp at the sport they were was planned by God because that would tell Pharaoh that the Israelites had no intention of coming back to Egypt. Oh, did you forget? The deal Moses had with Pharaoh was that they would go into the wilderness on a three-day journey and worship God (Exodus 3:18; 5:3; 8:27). Let's think from the side of Pharaoh. If they traveled for three days, worship God for three days, they would travel three days back to Egypt, or something like that (made up, blah!). What I am trying to say here is that Pharaoh expected the Israelites to come back to Egypt, but that wasn't God's or Moses' intention. Is that a misrepresentation? On whose part is it?

Anyway, the Israelites saw Pharaoh's chariots, and they embraced fear, cried out to Moses as if he was their father, questioned him, and desired to go back to slavery. Where is the boldness they left with? It's all gone suddenly. I need you to know this—doing what God wants you to do doesn't mean everything will be perfect or go smoothly, but amid the challenges, put your trust in God. You should continue to work by faith and not by sight. There are fearful things/ to shake us every time, meaning, everyone will be fearful at one point or the other. But, how you deal with it matters. You should also know that God is with you, and He has not given you a spirit of fear, but of power and of love and of a sound mind (2 Timothy 1:7).

Quiz 23
Read Exodus 14:13-24.

1.Moses said to the scared Israelites that they should not be afraid, they should stand still and see the salvation of the Lord, which He will accomplish for them. Then He said another thing to them. What was that?

    a. The Egyptians you see today will die in the Red Sea.

    b. The Egyptians you see today, you should mourn for them.

    c. The Egyptians you see today are nothing but shadows.

    d. The Egyptians you see today, you shall see them no more.

2. One last thing Moses said to the people was _____.

    a. The Lord is with you.

    b. The Lord is the Most High.

    c. Lord is Lord. You should know this.

    d. The Lord will fight for you, and you shall hold your peace.

3. Moses left the Children of Israel and cried to the Lord, and God asked Moses, "Why are you crying to Me? Tell the Children of Israel to _____."

    a. Go forward.

    b. Keep quiet.

    c. Pack their baggage and be ready to fight back.

    d. Lower their voices, so Pharoah will not know that they fear him.

4. "Why are you crying to Me?" the Lord asked Moses in Exodus 14:15. The Red Sea was in front of the Israelites. Pharaoh and

his army were behind them, and the mountain was beside them. The people were scared to death, and they cried to Moses, who calmed them down. Moses gave them confidence in God and told them they didn't have to be afraid but to stand still and see the salvation of the Lord. Now the Lord is asking Moses why he was crying to Him. What could Moses be doing that warranted this question from God?

5. The Lord also asked Moses to lift his rod, _____.
a. Ask the Israelites to look at it as they pray to Him
b. Stretch out his hand over the sea and divide it.
c. Swing it around his head seven times and use it to wipe the sea.
d. Throw it up and use it to hide the sea's waters.

6. The result of Moses' action was that, _____.
a. The Children of Israel could cross the sea on dry ground.
b. The Children of Israel could cross the sea on dry ground and pick up the fish on the ground.
c. The Children of Israel became respectful of the Lord.
d. The Children of Israel waved goodbye to the Egyptians one last time.

7. All this while, the Lord's angel, who goes before the Children of Israel, in a pillar of cloud by day and of fire by night, left their front, went behind them, and stayed between the Hebrews and the Egyptians. It gave cloud and darkness to the Egyptians and gave light by night to the Israelites. This happened for a reason. Why did it happen?
a. So the Hebrews can go from the Egyptians
b. So the fearful Israelites will not go and join the Egyptians
c. So the Hebrews will not surrender to the Egyptians
d. So there will be a distance between them

8. Moses stretched his hand as the Lord had told him to. The Lord caused the sea to go back by a strong wind all night and made the sea into dry land. What type of wind did the Lord use?
a. East wind
b. West wind
c. North wind
d. South wind

9. The Children of Israel went through the sea on dry ground, and the water was a protection and an entertaining sight to them on both sides. Is that true or false?

10. The Egyptians pursued the Hebrews and went into the midst of the sea on the dry path the Lord had made. In the morning, the Lord looked down upon the army of the Egyptians through_ _ _ _ _, and He troubled them.
   a. The reflection of the sea
   b. Jesus
   c. A glass
   d. The pillar of cloud and fire

God Uses Anything!
Have you noticed something since we started this Exodus? God has been using elements to accomplish His purpose. During the plagues, He turned water into blood, He made dust (earth) turned to lice (Exodus 8:17), Moses took ashes from a furnace, scattered them towards Heaven in the sight of Pharaoh and it became fine dust that turned to boils (Exodus 9:9), God made east wind (air) to bring locust and used the west wind to remove them (Exodus 10:13, 18). He led them on their journey with a pillar of cloud by day and that of fire by night (Exodus 14:24). Here in the crossing of the Red Sea, He used wind, fire (at night), earth (dry ground), and water, ha, ha, ha. He used all four of them at once! Praise our God! What is left?

I need you to take four different containers or anything that can hold counting stuff, like beads, stones, etc. Label them wind, water, earth, and fire. Any time you notice we talked about God doing His marvelous works using any of them, you just take one of your counters and place it in the container. Are you ready? You know, He created them, right? He can use them anytime He wants. Say Halleluiah to God!

Quiz 24
Read Exodus 14:24-31; 15:1-2.

1.When the Lord looked through the pillar of cloud and fire on the Egyptians, He _____.
   a. Confused them.
   b. Set a differentiation between them.
   c. Took their chariot's wheels off.
   d. Made the road gallop.

2. The protective Lord made the Egyptians' chariot's wheels fall off. When the Egyptians realized they could not ride fast, they advised themselves to _____.
   a. Run away from Israel's face, for the Lord fights for His people and against Egypt.
   b. Pull even harder because they are so close to them.
   c. Separate so half of them can go back in case the sea returns.
   d. Go back, for they cannot catch up with them.

3. The Lord asked Moses to _____ so the water would fall back onto the Egyptians' chariots and horse riders.
   a. Raise his rod to the sky.
   b. Stretch out his hand over the sea.
   c. Wave his rod sideways.
   d. Use his rod to hide the dry path.

4. Moses stretched his hand over the sea, and in the morning, the water covered the Egyptians. So the Lord saved Israel that day from their enemies, and they looked at their dead enemies from the seashore. That day, the Israelites feared the Lord, _____.
   a. And believed Him
   b. And believed Moses
   c. Believed Him and His servant Moses

d. And believed whatever Moses told them to

5. When Moses and the Children of Israel saw what God had done for them, they _____.
a. Poured dust on their bodies unto the Lord in celebration
b. Sang unto the Lord
c. Prayed unto God
d. Knelt in worship

6. I will sing unto the Lord, for He has triumphed _____.
a. Gloriously
b. Righteously
c. Miraculously
d. Perfectly

7. The Lord is my strength and _____.
a. Victory
b. Safety
c. Song
d. Hope

8. And He has become my _____.
a. Strength
b. Song
c. Hope
d. Salvation

9. He is my God, and I will _____.
a. Exalt Him
b. Praise Him
c. Worship Him
d. Bow down before Him

10. My father's God and I will _____.
a. Exalt Him
b. Praise Him
c. Worship Him
d. Bow down before Him

Singing Unto God!

Do you sing at all? Many people don't enjoy singing. They think about how their voices will sound before others. But, you know what? You are not singing to please people, but God. He created you and He wants to hear you sing praise to Him all the time. David was also a wonderful singer. Some people have rusty, smooth, beautiful voices, etc. God created them and loved them all. I challenge you to sing unto God, who made you in His image. Do not think about those around you when you do.

Circle the picture of things that were present during the crossing of the red sea that was mentioned.

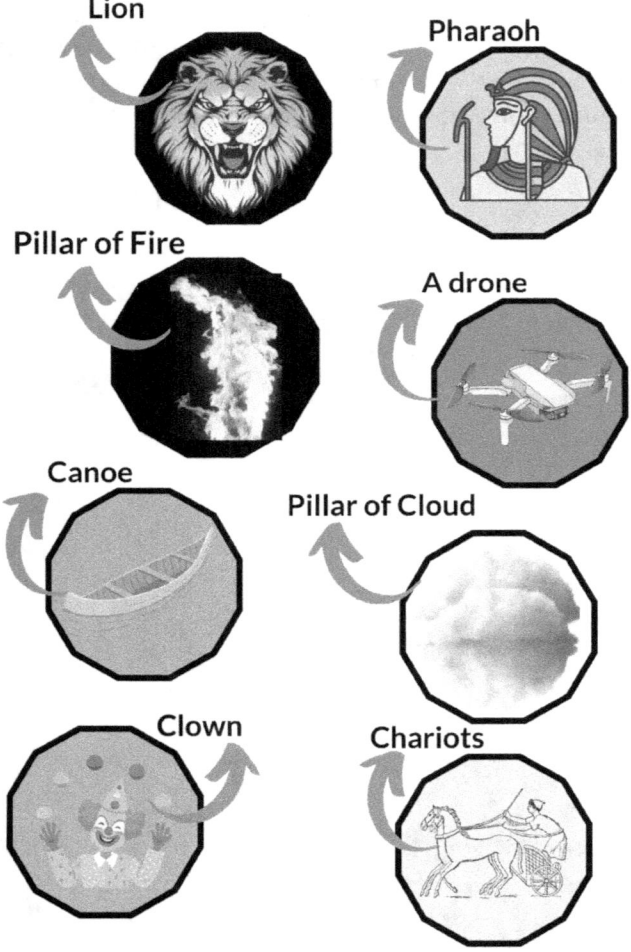

Quiz 25
Read Exodus 15:3-11.

1.The Lord is a man of _____.
   a. War
   b. Justice
   c. Violence
   d. Destruction

2. Your right hand, O Lord, has become _____.
a. Mighty
b. Victorious
c. Success
d. Glorious in power

3. Your right hand, O Lord, has dashed _____.
a. The enemy in the water
b. The enemy in their grave
c. The enemy in pieces
d. The enemy in silence

4. And in the greatness of Your excellence, You have overthrown those who rose against _____.
a. Us
b. Your children
c. You
d. Your firstborn

5. You sent Your _____.
a. Wrath
b. Justice
c. Destruction
d. Sword

6. It consumed them like _____.
a. Grass
b. Weed
c. Food
d. Stubble

7. And with the blast of Your _____.
a. Breath
b. Nostrils
c. Anger
d. Wrath

8. The waters were gathered _____.
a. Together
b. In heaps
c. Scattered
d. Warm

9. The enemy said I will _____ and I will _____.
a. Pursue, overtake
b. Pursue, be victorious
c. Pursue, bring them back to slavery
d. Pursue, destroy them

10. Who is like ____, O Lord, among the ___?
a. Us, earth
b. Us, inhabitants of the earth
c. Us, Your creation
d. You, gods

Singing and Dancing!

Here is Moses and the Children of Israel still singing and giving praise to God. Below is a very popular song written from this Exodus 15:11.
Who is like You, O Lord, among the gods?
Who is like You, glorious in holiness,
Fearful in praises, doing wonders?

Quiz 26

Read Exodus 15:11-26.

Who is like You, glorious in _____, fearful in _____, doing _____?
    a. Holiness, praises, wonders
    b. Victory, justice, miracles
    c. Faithfulness, action, justice
    d. Protection, deliverance, wonders

2. Miriam, the sister of Moses, was a _____.
    a. Princess
    b. Prophetess
    c. Fighter
    d. Cook

3. Miriam took the timbrel in her hand, and the women took eggshells and danced. Is that true or false?

4. Moses brought the Children of Israel into the wilderness of _____.
    a. Meriba
    b. Shur
    c. Ai
    d. The plain

5. How many days did they travel before they arrived at Shur?
    a. Two days
    b. Three days
    c. Four days
    d. Five days

6. In the wilderness of Shur, the Israelites did not find _____.
    a. Water

b. Shelter

c. Food

d. Animals

7. Israel came to _____ and could not drink the water of the place.

a. Marah

b. Meribah

c. Leach

d. East desert

8. Israel could not drink the water of Marah because _____.

a. The water was salty.

b. The water was bitter.

c. The water was sugary.

d. The water was bloody.

9. The people complained against Moses, asking him what they shall drink, and he cried unto the Lord, who showed him something that he could throw into the water to make it sweet for drinking. What did God show Moses?

a. A stone

b. A herb

c. A tree

d. A rose

10. There, the Lord told the Israelites that if they obeyed and kept His commandments, He would put none of the diseases He had placed on the Egyptians on them because He is the Lord who _____.

a. Destroys them

b. Heals them

c. Rescued them

d. Delivered them

Look for the Good in People!

How many days did the Children of Israel that were singing and dancing unto the Lord after saving them from Pharaoh stay before they forgot about what He has done for them because they could not drink water? Three days! Does that surprise you? We do that sometimes, too. When we ask for a favor from our parents and they granted it to us, we might ask another, and when they say no, we become angry. It's the same with the Israelites. How do we overcome this? Always look for the good in every situation. When something is happening, ask yourself, what are the positives that could come out of this? When you stop finding faults, you will be more grateful to God and will appreciate others more. Will you try that?

Quiz 27
Read Exodus 15:27; 16:1-6.

1.What was one of Moses' strengths?

2. Then Israel moved to a place where there were twelve wells of water and seventy palm trees. They camped there beside the waters. What is the name of that place?
a. Merraa
b. Elim
c. Zoah
d. Timm

3, The Hebrews journeyed from Elim and came to _____.
a. The wilderness of Sinai
b. The wilderness of Sin
c. The wilderness for Throne
d. The wilderness of Mothers

4. The wilderness of Sin is between Elim and Mothers. Is that true or false?

5. The Israelites arrived in the wilderness of Sin between Elim and Sanai on the _____ day of the second month after they departed Egypt.
a. Twelfth
b. Thirteenth
c. Fourteenth Exodus

d. Fifteenth

6. The people complained to Moses and Aaron that it would have been better if they had died by the hand of the Lord in Egypt, where they had meat and ate bread because Moses had brought them into the wilderness to kill them with _____.
a. The heat of the sun
b. The stress of walking
c. Loneliness
d. Hunger

7. God told Moses He would give the Children of Israel bread, but that the bread would come from _____.
a. The east wind
b. The west wind
c. The forest
d. Heaven

8. God said to Moses that He wanted to know if the people would obey His law. He told Moses what he should tell the Children of Israel–they should take only what they could finish each day, but on the _____ day, they could take doubled potion.
a. Third
b. Fourth
c. Fifth
d. Sixth

9. Moses said to the people that in the evening, they would know that the Lord God had brought them out of the house of bondage (Egypt), and in the morning, they shall see something because He hears their whining. What will they see in the morning?
a. Food
b. Water
c. The glory of the Lord
d. Dews

10. Moses also said that the Lord would give them _____ in the morning and _____ to eat in the evening.
a. Meat, pizza
b. Bread, meat

c. Pizza, vegetable
d. Lasagna, meat

Do You Ask Or Complain?

The Israelites complained about Moses bringing them to die of hunger, then God promised to give them what they want.

Note that there is a difference between asking for something and complaining about something. The Israelites didn't ask but complained. Look at the statement below and pick the complaining one from the asking one.

Moses, you have brought us out into this wilderness to kill this whole assembly with hunger.

Moses, we need food because we are starving.

Yes..., which one is the complaining one? The first one. Good job!

We would love to see many other children being taught God's truths in their homes. If we were valuable to you in that way, please leave an honest review on Amazon or your bookstore, and it will encourage other parents to teach their children about God—with our help.

Quiz 28
Read Exodus 16:7-31; 17:1-6.

1.Moses asked Aaron to speak to the people that they should come close to the Lord because He had heard their complaints. While Aaron was speaking, they looked towards the wilderness and saw _____.
   a. The glory of God in the cloud
   b. Food
   c. Eagles
   d. Angels with drawn swords

2. Just as the Lord had said, some birds came and covered the camp in the evening. What was the name of the birds?
   a. Doves
   b. Quails
   c. Chickens
   d. Turkeys

3. In the morning, when the dew left, they found some round substance as fine as frost on the ground. They did not know what it was. Moses told them it was bread the Lord had given them to eat. They called the bread _____.
   a. Frosty
   b. White bread
   c. Manna
   d. Buns

4. Moses said they should take only what they could eat each day, but some took more than enough, and in the morning, _____.
   a. It turned to dough
   b. It became hard
   c. It became black

d. It bred worms and stank.

5. Moses was unhappy, so they gathered it every morning, and when the sun became hot, the manna _____.
a. Spread
b. Melted
c. Rises
d. Stank

6. The seventh day was called the glorious or memorable day. Is that true or false?

7. The manna was white like coriander seed, and they described its taste as _____.
a. Honey garlic
b. Wafers made with honey
c. Bread made with honey
d. Pizza

8. The Lord said they should keep an omer of the manna for generations to come. The Children of Israel ate manna for _____.
a. Thirty years
b. Forty years
c. Fifty years
d. Sixty years

9. The Israelites journeyed from Sin's Wilderness and camped at _____ with no water.
a. Sanai
b. Mopet
c. Delve
d. Rephidim

10. Again, the people complained Moses had brought them from Egypt to kill their children and livestock of thirst. Moses cried to the Lord, saying they were almost ready to stone him. The Lord told him He would stand before him in _____, before a rock. Moses should use the rod he used in dividing the Red Sea to strike the rock, and water would come out so the people could drink.

a. Sanai
b. Horeb
c. Media
d. Rephidim

Thirsty!

In the quiz before this one, the Israelites complained about Moses bringing them to perish of hunger, then God provided manna for them. When they arrived at Rephidim, they started complaining of thirst. What do you notice in the last question? Did you notice how God uses those elements to supply the Israelites' needs? Name them. Yeah! Rock (earth) and water. Now grab your containers and put one stone each in the two elements. I told yah, God is the elements' creator. Hurrah for God!

Okay, grab your containers again! The Lord gave the Israelites quails to eat in this quiz as well. The account in this Exodus didn't show how the quails arrived at the camp, but Numbers 11:31-33 says it was a wind that went from the Lord that brought the quails to the camp. Don't forget that because we will talk more about it in the fourth series of this book—Numbers. Now you throw one of your counting materials into your container of wind.

Quiz 29
Read Exodus 17:7-16; 18:1-5.

1.At Horeb, Moses did according to what the Lord had said to him in the presence of the people, and water came out. He called the name of the place _____ because of the people's contention as they tempted the Lord God, saying, "Is the Lord among us or not?" (Exodus 17:7).
   a. Massah and Meribah
   b. Meribah and Horeb
   c. Meribah and Sadness
   d. Meribah and Contention

2. God gave the Israelites bread from Heaven (manna) in the wilderness. They were to gather only what they could eat each day, but they would pick twice the amount on the sixth day. God asked Moses to tell Aaron to fill an Omar with manna so he could lay it before the Lord and keep it for generations. There is something different between the manna, the Children of Israel gathered every day and the manna Aaron kept. What is the difference?

3. The Exodus account of the pot Aaron kept the manna doesn't reveal its look, but Hebrews 9:4 does. What kind of pot did Aaron keep the manna in?

4. At Rephidim, the Midianites came to fight against the Children of Israel. Is that true or false?

5. When the Amalekites came to fight against the Israelites, Moses said to _ _ _ _ _ to choose some men and fight against them.
a. Joshua
b. Aaron
c. Hur
d. Termer

6. Moses asked Joshua to choose some men to go with him and fight against the Amalekites while he stood on top of the hill with the rod of God in his hand. Joshua did according to what Moses said, and Moses held his hands up, but when Moses' hands were tired, and he dropped them, the Amalekites started winning. Aw! That was not good for the Israelites. Two people went to help Moses with his hands. Who were those people?
a. Phinehas and Lead
b. Phinehas and Hur
c. Aaron and Hur
d. Aaron and Lead

7. When Moses' hands were tired, Aaron and Hur put something under Moses' hands on both sides, so they were steady until nighttime. That was how Joshua defeated the Amalekites. What did they put under Moses' hands?
a. A log
b. A stone
c. A chair
d. A pillow

8. The Lord asked Moses to write and say it in the hearing of Joshua that He will utterly blot out the remembrance of Amalek from under Heaven because they fought with the Israelites. Then Moses built an altar and called its name _ _ _ _ _ _.
a. The-Lord-Is My-Guide

b. The-Lord-Is-My-Banner
c. The-Lord-Is-Here
d. The-Lord-Is-Good

9. When the Hebrews became thirsty and complained to Moses, God told Moses to take some elders of Israel and go to the rock at Horeb and that He would stand before him on the rock. He asked Moses to strike the rock so water could come out for the Children of Israel to drink (Exodus 17:6). Moses did as God commanded him to, and water came out. Hurrah! The Lord stood upon the rock; therefore, Moses struck the Lord when he struck the rock! What does this signify?

10. Jethro, who is Ruel, the priest of Midian, Moses' father-in-law, heard all that the Lord God had done for Moses and the Israelites when bringing them out of Egypt. He took Zipporah, her two sons, and came to meet Moses where he was camping at _____.
a. The wilderness of Midian
b. The wilderness of the Amalekites
c. The Mountain of God
d. The Mountain of the Amalekites

Teamwork ha?

What did you notice with Moses, Aaron, Hur, and Joshua? Teamwork, right? God did not make human beings to be by themselves. I think that was why He made Eve for Adam. If Moses had said I would do this myself, his people would die. If Aaron or Hur said, oh no, Moses didn't respect me the way I wanted him to, so I will not assist him in keeping his hand up, the Israelites would die. What about Joshua? If he had refused to war with the Amalekites, the Children of Israel would be killed. Teamwork is very important. God wants us to be excellent team players. Oooh! Here is an example of how God commanded the parents and children to be good team players. God wants you, kids, to ask your parents questions about His works. When you do, your parents will tell you about His great works (Exodus 12:26-27). Do you know the result of that? You write the Word of God in your heart, for Psalm 45:1 says your tongue is the pen of a ready writer. Also, you will help your family to think and remember the goodness of God. There are different places in the Bible where God asked us to remember things, for example, Exodus 13:3. When you bring this idea outside the Bible, you know that asking questions helps someone to think about something they wouldn't have thought about. I challenge you today to consciously ask your parents questions. Don't be scared of it.

Quiz 30
Read Exodus 18:6-27; 19:1-13.

1.Jethro brought Zipporah and her two sons to Moses. They rejoiced and asked each other about their well-being, then Jethro offered a _ _ _ _ _ and other sacrifices unto the Lord.
   a. Sin offering
   b. Coming out of Egypt offering
   c. Praise offering
   d. Burnt offering

2. Aaron came with the elders of Israel to eat bread with Jethro. Is that true or false?

3. Moses was the judge of the people all this while, but someone advised him to take from among the men, men that fear God, are truthful, hate covetousness, and place them over the rulers of thousands, hundreds, fifties, and tens so they can judge the people. All this was to make it easier for Moses. Who was the person who gave Moses this advice?
   a. Aaron
   b. Joshua
   c. Jethro
   d. Zipporah

4. In the third month, after the Israelites had left Egypt, they came to a wilderness. What is the name of the wilderness?
   a. Wilderness of Sin
   b. Wilderness of Horeb
   c. Wilderness of Reuel
   d. Wilderness of Sinai

5. When the Israelites arrived in the wilderness of Sinai, they camped _ _ _ _ _ _.

a. Before the mountain

b. Before the twenty-nine trees

c. Before the wells

d. Before the blessed seven hills

6. The Lord said to Moses that He did something to bring Israel to Himself. What was that?

a. He carried them on horses.

b. He carried them on camels.

c. He bore them on eagle's wings.

d. He took them on a chariot of fire.

7. God also told Moses that he should tell the Israelites that they shall be _____ if they keep His commandments.

a. A kingdom of priests and a holy nation

b. An empire of the saint and everlasting nation

c. A domain of supermen and a nation of nations

d. A kingdom of the blessed and a supernatural nation

8. When Moses shared what the Lord had told him, the people said, "_____."

a. The Lord already blesses us, and we will serve Him forever.

b. We are blessed above all nations.

c. We will obey the Lord so long as it is convenient for us

d. All that the Lord has said, we will do.

9. The Lord told Moses He would come down to Mount Sinai on the _____ day, so Moses should tell the people to wash their clothes and consecrate themselves.

a. Second

b. Third

c. Fourth

d. Fifth

10. Moses told the people that when the Lord comes to the mountain, no one or beast shall touch it; whoever did (man or beast) shall be killed. What was the manner of death Moses set for the beast or man that disobeyed?

a. Stoned or buried alive

b. Stoned or banished

c. Stoned or shot with an arrow

d. Stoned or beaten to death

God Uses People to Help Us!

When Moses went back to Egypt, he took his wife and two sons with him. He later sent them back, the reason for that is not given in the Bible. Here, we see his father-in-law, Jethro, bringing his wife and two sons back to him. He offered a burnt offering unto God. This Jethro was the one that advised Moses to have levels of government. Before his coming, Moses was handling all the cases — big or small by himself. Do you know something I learned from this? God always uses people to help us. Jethro advised Moses, and he took his advice. Here, Moses had a choice either to heed his father-in-law's advice or not. As you live your life, different people will give you different advice at different times. You should be able to listen and discern the advice that is backed up by the Word of God from the advice that is coming from the pit of hell. You have the Spirit of God in you, and He will help you with that.

Quiz 31
Read Exodus 19:14-25; 20:1-5.

1.On the third day, in the morning, there was thunder, lightning, and a thick cloud on the mountain, then the sound of a very loud trumpet, and the people in the camp were scared. Moses brought the people to the mountain, and when they reached there, it was filled with _____.
   a. Fire
   b. Smoke
   c. Snow
   d. Lightning

2. What is the longest recorded miracle in the Bible?

3. The mountain was in smoke when the Children of Israel arrived at its foot. Why?
   a. Because the Lord descended upon it in fire
   b. Because the Lord descended upon it in smoke
   c. Because the Lord descended upon it in snow
   d. Because the Lord descended upon it in lightning

4. Apart from the smoke on the mountain, something else was happening on it. What was it?
   a. It quaked.
   b. It snowed.
   c. Volcano eruption
   d. Heat

5. Moses spoke unto God at the mountain, and He answered him by thunder and lightning. Is that true or false?

6. When Moses went up the mountain, the Lord asked him to go down and warn the people less they come near it, but Moses told Him the people would not because he had warned them and set boundaries on it. He told Moses to go and bring _____ with him.
    a. Aaron
    b. Joshua
    c. Hur
    d. Eliezer

7. The Lord did what He did because He wanted the people to _____.
    a. Obey the Him
    b. Believe Moses forever
    c. See His glory
    d. Know He existed

8. God gave Moses the Ten Commandments for the Israelites on Mount Sinai. What was the first commandment?
    a. You shall have no other gods before Me.
    b. Do not take the name of the Lord your God in vain.
    c. Remember the Sabbath day and keep it holy.
    d. Honor your father and mother.

9. God said to Moses that the Israelites shall have no other gods before Him and shall not make any carved image and worship it. He gave a reason for this. What was the reason He gave?
    a. He is a God that does not tolerate.
    b. He is a God of justice.
    c. He is a jealous God.
    d. He is a consuming fire.

10. What is the second commandment?
    a. You shall have no other gods before Me.
    b. You shall not make for yourselves a carved image. You shall not bow down to them nor serve them.
    c. Remember the Sabbath day and keep it holy.
    d. Honor your father and mother.

God Uses Anything!

Oooh! Elements! Elements!! Elements!!! Which container are you going to put these in? Yes! Fire! The entire mountain was in smoke because God descended upon it on fire! (Exodus 19:18). Again, the mountain quaked in the same verse. What was that element? Earth! Correct! God again used earth here.

Quiz 32
Read Exodus 20:5-17.

1.The Lord cursed anyone who broke the 2nd Commandment, even to the third and fourth generations. That same curse was repeated in Exodus 34:7 and Numbers 14:18. God took this curse away in Ezekiel 18:1-4 and Jeremiah 31:29-34. Jeremiah put an end to this curse and spoke a prophecy for us. What did Jeremiah prophesy about?

2. What is the third commandment?
a. You shall have no other gods before Me
b. You shall not make for yourself a carved image, you shall not bow down to them or serve them.
c. You shall not take the name of the Lord your God in vain.
d. Honor your father and mother.

3. What is the fourth commandment?
a. You shall have no other gods before Me.
b. Do not take the name of the Lord your God in vain.
c. Remember the Sabbath day and keep it holy.
d. Honor your father and mother.

4. What is the fifth commandment?.
a. Honor your father and mother.
b. You shall not kill.
c. You shall not steal.
d. You shall not bear false witness against your neighbor.

5. What is the sixth commandment?
a. You shall not kill.
b. You shall not commit adultery.
c. You shall not steal.
d. You shall not bear false witness against your neighbor.

6. What is the seventh commandment?
a. Honor your father and mother.
b. You shall not commit adultery.
c. You shall not steal.
d. You shall not bear false witness against your neighbor.

7. What is the eight commandments?
a. Honor your father and mother.
b. You shall not commit adultery.
c. You shall not steal.
d. You shall not bear false witness against your neighbor.

8. What is the ninth commandment?
a. You shall not steal.
b. You shall not bear false witness against your neighbor.
c. You shall not covet your neighbor's house.
d. You shall not covet your neighbor's wife.

9. What is the tenth commandment?
a. You shall not steal.
b. You shall not bear false witness against your neighbor.
c. You shall not kill.
d. You shall not covet your neighbor's wife or house.

10. God gave the Israelites the Ten Commandments, but they could not keep them. We can't either. There is nothing wrong with the commandments, though, but we can't attain them because of our fallen and sinful nature (Romans 7:12-13). We don't need to worry about having to keep the Ten Commandments

in the New Covenant. Phew! What a relief! We only have one commandment to keep. What is the command we need to keep?

Quiz 33
Read Exodus 20:18-26; 21:1-20.

When the people heard all that was happening–the thundering, the lightning, the sound of the trumpet, and the smoky mountain, they said to Moses that he should speak with them they would listen. They also said the Lord should not talk with them directly because something would happen to them. What were they afraid of?
a. They will be blind.
b. They will die.
c. They will not hear.
d. They will be deaf.

2. Moses told the people not to be afraid because God had come to show His glory, presence, and existence to them. Is that true or false?

3. God told Moses the people had seen Him talking with him from Heaven. Now, they shall make an altar of earth and offerings for Him. What offerings did God talk about here?
a. Burnt and peace offerings
b. Burnt and sin offerings
c. Burnt and attornment offering
d. Burnt and forgiveness offering

4. God gave them some laws to help them in their day-to-day living. He said if they buy a Hebrew servant, he shall serve the buyer for _____.
a. Four years
b. Five years
c. Six years
d. Seven years

5. If an enslaved person comes into slavery by himself, he shall go out by himself. If he comes in married, he shall go out with his wife. If the master gave him a wife and he had children, when he leaves, what will happen to those children?

a. He shall go with the children.

b. The children shall decide if they will go with their father or stay with their father's master.

c. The children shall belong to the master.

d. The children shall be sold, then the master and the servant shall have an equal share of the money.

6. Anyone that kills a man shall be killed. Is that true or false?

7. Whoever strikes his father or mother shall be?

a. Banished

b. Punished

c. Fined

d. Killed

8. Whoever kidnaps a person shall be _____?

a. Banished

b. Punished

c. Fined

d. Killed

9. Whoever cursed his father or mother shall be killed. Is that true or false?

10. If a man beats his female or male servant with a rod and they die, that person shall be _____?

a. Banished

b. Punished

c. Fined

d. Killed

Love One Another!

Here, God is still giving the Children of Israel rules. Jesus summarizes all these rules into two: "You shall love the Lord your God with all your hearts, with all your soul, and with all you mind." This is the first commandment. The second he said, "You shall love your neighbor as yourself" (Mathew 22:37-39). He gave these before He died. After His resurrection, Jesus gave one commandment: "A new commandment I give to you, that you love one another; as I have loved you" (John 13:34; 15:12.)

You may wonder, why one? Those who abide in love abide in God (1 John 4:16), for God is love (1 John 4:8).

Quiz 34
Read Exodus 21:21-36; 22:1-2.

1.God provided manna for the Israelites all their days in the wilderness until the day after they _____.

2. If a man beats a woman with a child and she gives birth prematurely, but no harm follows, he shall be punished as the woman's husband determines, but if there is harm, there shall be a punishment for the man. What is the punishment?
a. Life for life, eye for an eye, tooth for tooth, hand for hand, foot for foot, burn for burn, wound for wound, and stripe for stripe
b. Banished forever
c. Fined as the woman's husband wants
d. Flogged and fined as the husband chooses

3. If a man strikes his male or female servant and loses one of their eyes, or he strikes their tooth, and they lose their tooth, he shall _____.
a. Sell them
b. Kill them
c. Let them go free
d. Be with him until they die

4. If an ox kills a human being, the people shall stone the ox to death, and its flesh shall not be eaten. Is that true or false?

5. Something shall happen to the owner of an ox that kills a person. What shall happen to him?
a. He shall be banished.
b. He shall be fined.
c. He shall be acquitted.
d. He shall be punished.

6. If a man dug a pit and did not cover it and an animal fell into it, the digger of the pit shall _____.
a. Eat the dead animal.
b. Burn the dead animal.
c. Give the owner of the dead animal money, and the dead one shall be his.
d. Be banished.

7. If an ox hurts another man's ox and it dies, they shall sell the live one, and _____.
a. They shall share the proceeds
b. They shall give it to the poor
c. They shall give it to the priest
d. They shall put it on the altar

8. If an ox tended to thrust in times past, and the owner did not keep it confined, and it killed another ox, something shall be done to the owner of that ox. What shall be done to him?
a. Banished
b. Killed
c. Pay ox for ox. He shall take the dead one and give his ox to the owner of the dead ox.
d. Fined

9. If a man steals an ox or sheep and slaughters or sells it, he shall pay five oxen for an ox and four sheep for a sheep. Is that true or false?

10. There is no bloodshed for one that killed a (an) _____.
a. Adulterer
b. Adulteress
c. Thief breaking in
d. Murderer

God, Love His Creation!

Those are some regulations about animals and property. God is concerned about everything. You should be, too.

Quiz 35
Read Exodus 22:3-30.

1.If the thief is caught alive and what he stole is found in his hand, he shall restore how many times what he stole?
   a. Double
   b. Three times
   c. Seven times
   d. Nine times

2. If the thief can't restore double what he has stolen, they shall kill him. Is that true or false?

3. There is a kind of sinful people that should not be permitted to live. What kind of activity is that?
   a. A prophet
   b. A sorceress
   c. A lier
   d. A deceiver

4. Whoever lies with an animal shall be _____.
   a. Banished
   b. Killed
   c. Fined
   d. Suspended

5. Whoever sacrifices to other gods shall be banished. Is that true or false?

6. One law said the Israelites should not mistreat a stranger or oppress them. Why?
   a. Strangers will always be everywhere.
   b. There is a blessing in treating strangers well.
   c. They were strangers in Egypt.

d. Strangers can be heavenly beings sometimes.

7. God told them not to afflict the widows and fatherless. If they are poorly treated, and they cry to Him, He will hear their cry, and His wrath will become hot, then He will _____.
a. Afflict them
b. Punish them
c. Kill them with the sword; their wives shall be widows and their children, fatherless
d. Send them to slavery

8. They shall _____ if they lend money to anyone poor.
a. Allow the borrower to pay gradually.
b. Not collect interest
c. Ask the borrower to pay half.
d. Tell the borrower not to pay back the money they borrowed.

9. They shall not revile God or _____ the ruler of their people.
a. Curse
b. Talk behind
c. Accuse
d. Support

10. They shall give the firstborn of their sons to God, and they shall do the same thing with their oxen and sheep. The animals shall be with their mother for_____ days, and on the _____ day, they shall give it to God.
a. Five, seven
b. Seven, eight
c. Ninth, eleven
d. Five, eight

More Rules!

Continuation of rules. Remember, we only have one rule. In observing our one rule, we are technically living all these rules that were given to the Israelites. For example, if you love your friend, you will not steal his things. If you love your friend, you will not bear false witness against him.

How have things gone thus far? Give yourself a high five right now. Actually, you're doing fantastic. If you missed a few, don't worry, but you also don't have to give up. Read the Bible verse and respond to the questions. You'll make significant progress very soon. You are aware that everyone began where you are right now. You will learn more about it the more you read and listen to it. Well done!

Quiz 36
Read Exodus 22:31; 23:1-12.

1.They shall be holy men unto God, for they shall not eat meat that beasts in the field tear apart. What shall they do with the meat?
   a. Burn it by fire
   b. Bury it
   c. Give it to strangers
   d. Throw it to the dogs

2. The Israelites shall not _____ false reports.
   a. Be happy with
   b. Believe
   c. Think about
   d. Circulate

3. You shall not follow the crowd to _____.
   a. Do what is right
   b. Say what is honorable to their elders and the Lord their God
   c. Make an offering to the Lord God
   d. Do evil

4. They shall not be an unrighteous witness, and they shall not show partiality to a poor man. Is that true or false?

5. They shall do something to their enemy's ox or donkey going astray. What shall they do?
   a. Call a neighbor, who is not an enemy, to take it to the owner.
   b. Point them toward their owner.
   c. Give them water to drink.
   d. Take them back to the owner.

6. They should not kill the innocent or _____.
   a. Righteous

b. Young adults
c. Strangers
d. Travelers

7. God will not _ _ _ _ _ _ the wicked.
a. Forgive
b. Hear the prayers of
c. Justify
d. Show mercy to

8. God told them not to take a bribe. Why?
a. It blinds the discerning and perverts the words of the righteous.
b. Bribe money does not last long.
c. So He can hear their prayers when they pray to Him.
d. To prevent evil from among them.

9. The Lord told them to sow their land for _ _ _ _ _ years and allow it to rest for _ _ _ _ _year or years.
a. Five, six
b. Five, two
c. Six, one
d. Six, three

10. They shall do all their work in six days, and on the seventh day, they shall rest. Why?
a. So all that they have–animals and servants - may rest and be refreshed
b. To show how He made the world because He rested on the seventh day
c. Everything seven shall signify rest.
d. To make the rest part of their lives.

These are still a continuation of rules.

Quiz 37
Read Exodus 23:14-33.

1.God said they should keep several feasts to Him. How many feasts shall they keep to Him in a year?
   a. Two
   b. Three
   c. Four
   d. Five

2. What is the name of the feasts they would keep each year?
   a. Unleavened bread, Passover, and Victory
   b. Unleavened bread, Victory, and Thanksgiving
   c. Unleavened bread, Tabernacle, and Service
   d. Unleavened bread, Harvest, and Ingathering

3. Exodus 17:2 says, Therefore the people contended with Moses, and said, "Give us water, that we may drink." So, Moses said to them, "Why do you contend with me? Why do you tempt the Lord?" In Exodus 17:7, Moses called the name of the place Massah and Meribah because of the contention of the Children of Israel and because they tempted the Lord, saying, "Is the Lord among us or not?" Comparing verses 2 and 7 of Exodus 17, what does it mean to tempt the Lord?

4. The Lord told the Israelites to keep the Feast of Unleavened bread, known as the Passover, Harvest, and Ingathering. We know that the Feast of the Passover was to be celebrated for fourteen days starting on the fourteenth day in the month of Abib

when God passed over the houses of the Children of Israel and killed all the firstborn of both animals and humans in the land of Egypt. Here, God asked them to observe the Feast of Harvest. What then is this feast, anyway?

a. Thanksgiving to the Lord for giving them a fruitful harvest

b. Bringing the firstfruits of their labors they have sown in the fields to the Lord

c. Bringing the tenth of their harvest to the Lord

d. A and C above

5. Like the Feast of Unleavened Bread and Harvest, the Feast of Ingathering is done when they have gathered the fruit of their labors from the field. This Ingathering Feast has a set time for it to be celebrated. When is it done?

a. June

b. March

c. October

d. At the end of the year

6. Certain people shall appear before the Lord three times a year. Who shall do this?

a. Males

b. Females

c. Widows

d. Fatherless

7. The Lord told the Israelites that He had sent His angel before them to bring them into the land He had promised them. He said they should be aware of Him, hear His voice, and not provoke Him, because if they do, He will not forgive their sins. Why?

a. He guilts them.

b. He led them to where they were now.

c. His name is in Him.

d. He doesn't forgive; only God does.

8. If the Israelites obey the Lord, He will be a _____ to their enemies and a _____ to their adversaries.

a. Enemy and adversary

b. Spear and sword

c. Javelin and hindrance

d. Hindrance and killer

9. If the Children of Israel obey the Lord, His angel will go before them to the Amorites, Hittites, Perizzites, Canaanites, Hivites, and Jebusites that live in the land; then He will cut them off. The Israelites shall not _ _ _ _ _ to their gods, but they shall overthrow them, destroy them, and break down their sacred pillars.

a. Preserve them
b. Honor them
c. Take them home
d. Bow down

10. We learned the Amalekites attacked the Children of Israel at Rephidim (Exodus 17:8). Who were the Amalekites?

No Condition for Us. Yeah!

We saw the three feasts God commanded the Children of Israel to observe every year. The men, however, were to present themselves before the Lord three times, and we saw how God placed conditions for their protection. He would be an enemy to their enemies IF.... Now, we have the protection of God over our lives by grace, but we have to stay within the parameters for them to happen. This does not mean we have to work to receive the protection, but we know that whoever breaks through a wall will be bitten by a serpent (Ecclesiastic 10:8). We are under the protection of God, but if you leave it for any reason, there could or will be consequences. Maybe this analogy will make sense to you. I grew up in a rural area where people raise chickens in their yards. When a mother hen hashes her chicks, she takes them outside to feed. Sometimes eagles (maybe not eagles, but something like that) would fly about looking for chicks. When the mother hen sees the shadow of the flying eagle, she makes a sound for her chicks to come under her wings. Some will run to the mom, who will cover them with her wings. Some, however, will not, or because they were too far from the mother hen. The eagle would come and grab the chick and fly away. That is what I am talking about. We have to stay under the protection that God had provided for you and me for us to enjoy that, as stated in Psalm 91. I hope I was able to make things clear.

How are you doing so far? Are they too hard for yah? Are you getting better? I know it gets easier every time you try them. Come on! Let's continue!

Match the three-yearly Feasts

Passover Feast/ Unleavened Bread	The firstfruits of your labors which you have sown in the field
Feast of Ingathering	Done at the end of the year, when you have gathered in the fruit of your labors from the field
Feast of Harvest	Lamb without blemish (defect), Bitter Herbs, Unleavened Bread

Quiz 38
Read Exodus 23:25-33; 24:1-6.

1.What did the Amalekites do to the Israelites?

2. When the Israelites serve the Lord, He will bless them and give them bread and water, and He will also take _____ away from them.
   a. Sadness
   b. Death
   c. Tornado
   d. Sickness

3. If they obey Him, no one will suffer a miscarriage in the land, and He will _____.
   a. Carry them on an eagle's wing
   b. Fulfill the number of their days
   c. Watch them with His right hand
   d. Save them from all-natural disasters

4. God said He would send His fear before the Israelites and cause confusion among the people of the land they are going. He will send hornets before them to drive out the Hivites, Canaanites, and the Hittites. He will not drive them away in one year. He gave the reason for this. What is the reason He gave?
   a. The Israelites are unpredictable, and if He drives them away, they might be fearful.

b. The enemies should farm the land so He can drive them away when the harvest is ripe so the Israelites can harvest the crops they ran away from.

c. The land will become desolate, and the beast of the land will increase.

d. The people needed to be trained for warfare.

5. God set the boundaries of Israel from the Red Sea to Philistia, and from the desert to the river. He said He would deliver the people living in the land into the hands of the Israelites and would drive them away. He told them not to _____ with the people and their gods.

a. Be their friends

b. Make covenants

c. Take their houses

d. Follow their ways

6. Why did God say they should not make covenants with these people and their gods?

a. They will make them marry their ladies.

b. They will sin against Him by serving their gods and will be a snare to them.

c. They will make them stubborn.

d. They will make them lazy.

7. Here, they affirm the covenant. The Lord said to Moses, Aaron, Nadab, Abihu, and some group of people should come and worship. Who were those people?

a. The women

b. The widows

c. The children

d. The elders

8. Moses, Aaron, Nadab, Abihu, and the elders were to go and worship the Lord, but only one person shall come close. Who was that person?

a. Moses

b. Abihu

c. Nadab

d. Aaron

9. Moses spoke the Word of the Lord to the people, and they answered with one voice, saying all that the Lord had said they would do. Moses wrote everything down, built an altar at the foot of the mountain, and put twelve pillars there. Why did Moses place twelve pillars there?

    a. Twelve is an outstanding number

    b. Moses loved twelve

    c. According to the tribes (sons) of Israel

    d. To remember the month they were in

10. After Moses had built the altar, he sent young men, who offered a burnt offering and used one animal to sacrifice a peace offering to the Lord. What animal did they use?

    a. A young goat

    b. A young lamb

    c. A Sheep

    d. An Oxen

They Promised!

Here, the Children of Israel answered Moses with one voice saying, "All the words which the Lord has said we will do" (Exodus 24:3). I need you to pay a closer look to know if they kept to what they had said here.

Quiz 39
Read Exodus 24:6-17.

God promised the Israelites they would be His peculiar people IF... they obeyed and kept His commandments (Exodus 5). Under the New Covenant, God has made us a peculiar people and a holy nation, too (1 Peter 2:9). What is the difference between our promise and the Old Testament promise about being a peculiar people?

2. Moses took half of the blood and put it in basins, and the other half he sprinkled on the altar. Then he took one book and read it to the people. What book did Moses read?
   a. The Book of Peace Offering
   b. The Book of Burnt Offering
   c. The Book of the Covenant
   d. The Book of the Generations

3. After reading the book, Moses took the blood, sprinkled it on the people, and said _____.
   a. The blood of peace is on you.
   b. The blood of victory is on you.
   c. The blood of freedom is on you.
   d. This is the blood of the covenant which the Lord has made with you according to all these words.

4. Moses, Aaron, Nadab, Abihu, and seventy elders of Israel went up the mountain with Moses. These people saw the God

of Israel (feet), and they described what was under His feet. How did they describe it?

a. A pave work of sapphire stone like the very heavens in its clarity.

b. The whole earth was under His feet, and we saw what was happening in the camp.

c. Chariots of fire were under His feet, and they went around Him.

d. A glorious Host of Heaven was under His feet, and they sang, "Hallelujah," to the Lord who created Heaven and the earth.

5. God did not lay a hand on the nobles of Israel, and when they returned, they _____.

a. Drank and danced

b. Ate and drank

c. Worshipped God

d. Sang and danced

6. Moses went up to the mountain so God could give him stone tablets. What was his reason for going?

a. God invited him.

b. He wanted God to write everything for him so he could give them to the Children of Israel.

c. The elders of Israel sent him.

d. It was time for him to go.

7. When Moses was going to meet God for the tablets of stone, he went with _____.

a. Nadab

b. Abihu

c. Aaron

d. Joshua

8. Joshua was a nephew to Moses. Is that true or false?

9. Moses told the elders of Israel that he was leaving and that they should wait where they were until he returned. He asked them to meet _____ and _____ if they had any issues.

a. Aaron, Abihu

b. Aaron, Nadab

c.. Aaron, Hur

d. Aaron, Eliezer

10. When Moses went up the mountain, something covered it. What was that?
a. Cloud
b. Fire
c. Smoke
d. Thick darkness

They Saw God's Glory in Real-Time!

Aaron, his four sons, and the seventy elders of Israel practically saw the glory at the feet of God. They describe how it looks. Now, God had called Moses up the mountain, leaving the congregation of Israel under the care of Aaron and Hur. What now? Will they be able to keep the people faithful? Does seeing the glory of God able to help the seventy elders to stay faithful to God before the coming back of Moses? Will the children of Israel remain faithful to their agreement, "All that the Lord had said, we will do?" We will find out soon.

Quiz 40
Read Exodus 24:16-18; 25:1-8.

1. Moses went up the mountain, and the cloud covered it for several days because of the Glory of God, as seen by the Children of Israel. How many days did the cloud cover Mount Sinai?
   a. Five days
   b. Six days
   c. Seven days
   d. Eight days

2. When Moses was on the mountain, the cloud covered it for six days. On the seventh day, the Lord called Moses from the cloud. The Bible described the sight of God's glory. How was it described?
   a. A consuming fire
   b. A volcano eruption
   c. A smoky red blaze
   d. A tornado of fire

3. Moses was there on the mountain for forty-one days and nights. Is that true or false?

4. God told Moses to tell the Children of Israel to bring Him an offering, and He gave a condition for those that will to bring the offering. What was the condition He gave?
   a. Anyone that has a new wife only
   b. Anyone that has a new baby only
   c. Anyone who is willing with his heart only
   d. Everyone

5. One of the following lists is not what God said they should bring to Him as an offering.
   a. Gold, silver, bronze, blue, purple, and scarlet thread

b. Fine linen, goats' hair, ram skins dyed red, badger skins, and acacia wood

c. Logs of wood, axes, and livestock

d. Oil, spices, onyx stones, and stones

6. God asked them to bring oil, and there was a reason for that. What is the purpose of the oil?

a. For light

b. For anointing people

c. For anointing the altar

d. For boiling the incense

7. There was a reason for bringing the spice. What was the reason?

a. To make the place smell better

b. The spice smell will take away their body odor so they can smell better

c. For the anointing oil and the sweet incense

d. Sprinkle it on their burnt offerings

8. In Exodus 28:30, the Lord told Moses to put the Urim and Thummim on the breastplate, which was to be over Aaron's heart when he went in before the Lord. Their descriptions were not given, but they played an important role. (A) What were the Urim and Thummim used for in the Old Testament? (B) Name at least one person who used either the Urim, Thummim, or both.

9. God asked them to bring all these things because He wanted the Children of Israel to _____.

a. Work as team people just as He works with Jesus and the Holy Ghost

b. See how obedient they were

c. Build Him a sanctuary

d. Prepare for battle

10. There was a reason God wanted the Hebrews to build Him a sanctuary. What was that reason?
   a. So they can see Him all the time.
   b. So He could dwell among them.
   c. So they can have a place to worship Him.
   d. So He can rebuke them when they are out for evil.

On the Mountain!

Here, Moses was on top of the mountain along with Joshua, whom he took along with him. I know Joshua was far from where Moses was talking with God. What do you think?

Quiz 41
Read Exodus 25:9-14.

1.How did God give Moses the tabernacle's design and furnishing?
   a. He drew it for him.
   b. He showed him.
   c. He gave him the architectural design.
   d. He gave him the mini version for his reference.

2. The Children of Israel shall make an ark of silver and gold. Is that true or false?

3. What is the length of the ark?
   a. Two and a half cubits
   b. Two cubits
   c. Three cubits
   d. Three and a half cubits

4. What is the width of the ark?
   a. A cubit
   b. A cubit and half
   c. Two cubits
   d. Two and a half cubits

5. They shall overlay the ark with _____ both inside and outside.
   a. Pure silver
   b. Acacia wood
   c. Pure gold
   d. Pure gold and silver

6. The ark shall have a molding of gold all around it. Is that true or false?

7. During Aaron and his son's consecration, they put their hands on the head of one ram, and Moses killed the ram according to God's instructions. It became customary to touch an animal that must be sacrificed before it is slain, as directed by God Almighty. What does placing a hand on a sacrificial animal symbolize?

8. There shall be four rings of gold on the ark. Where shall they be placed?
a. The four sides
b. The four corners
c. Two on each long side
d. Two on each short side

9. They shall make poles of acacia wood and overlay them with
_____.
a. Silver
b. Gold
c. Bronze
d. Sweet incense

10. They shall place the poles _____ the sides of the ark.
a. On each corner
b. On each side
c. On top
d. Into the rings

The Temple in Heaven!

God showed Moses the design of the Tabernacle. Hmm..., what do you think? Yes, there is a Temple in Heaven and God showed Moses that temple so that he may build the one on earth to replicate that Heavenly one. In Exodus 25:40. That heavenly temple was the one Jesus entered when He made the ultimate sacrifice for the entire world, as recorded in Hebrews 9:23-25. God still told Moses to make the patterns to represent the designs that He showed him. This is really exceptional! Really! Oh, even in Hebrew 8:5, Paul repeated what God told Moses, who serve as the copy and shadow of the heavenly things, as Moses was divinely instructed when he was about to make the tabernacle. For He said, "See that you make all things according to the pattern shown you on the mountain." Did God take Moses to Heaven to see those designs, or did He bring the designs to earth for Moses to see? I don't know. What do you think?

Quiz 42
Read Exodus 25:14-21.

1.God asked Moses to make poles with acacia wood, overlay them with gold and place them inside the rings. There was a reason these poles should go inside the ring. What is the reason?
   a. It was a special design.
   b. Poles are a symbol of war.
   c. So they can easily carry them around.
   d. To hold it still.

2. They shall place _ _ _ _ _ in the ark.
   a. The testimony
   b. Moses' rod
   c. Manna
   d. All lost but found items

3. They shall also make a mercy seat. What will they use to make it?
   a. Pure gold
   b. Silver
   c. Acacia wood
   d. Bronze

4. The length of the mercy seat shall be three and a half cubits. Is that true or false?

5. Its width shall be _ _ _ _ _ _ _ _.
   a. One cubit
   b. One and a half cubit
   c. Two cubits
   d. Two and a half cubits

6. They shall make cherubim of hammered gold. How many cherubim shall they make?
a. Five
b. Four
c. Three
d. Two

7. Where shall they keep cherubim?
a. Two sides of the ark
b. Two ends of the mercy seat
c. In front of the ark
d. In front of the mercy seat

8. The cherubim shall stretch out their wings above the mercy seat, covering it, and they shall face _____.
a. The east of the tabernacle
b. The west tabernacle
c. Opposite each other
d. Face each other

9. They shall keep the mercy seat on top of the ark. Is that true or false?

10. Before Moses came back from the mountain with the Ten Commandments, the people had asked Aaron to make gods for them. Aaron made a calf for them, and they worshiped it. God was angry, and He said to Moses in Exodus 32:10, "Now, therefore, let Me alone, that My wrath may burn hot against them and I may consume them. And I will make you a great nation." Moses pleaded with the Lord, asking Him not to let His anger burn against His people and destroy them. He reminded God of His promise to Abraham, Isaac, and Jacob and told God that the Egyptians would hear and say He brought them out of Egypt to kill them. Hmm..., Moses did not let God kill them, even though God would have made a great nation out of him. What does this account tell you about Moses?

Heavenly Designs!

Remember that all these things—mercy seat, tabernacle, cherub (cherubim), etc, are Heavenly design things Moses saw with his eyes on the mountain.

Quiz 43
Read Exodus 25:22-40; 26:1.

They shall make a table of acacia wood. What shall be its length?
- a. One cubit
- b. One and a half cubit
- c. Two cubits
- d. Two and a half cubits

2. What shall be its width?
- a. One cubit
- b. One and a half cubit
- c. Two cubits
- d. Two and a half cubits

3. What shall be its height?
- a. One cubit
- b. One and a half cubit
- c. Two cubits
- d. Two and a half cubits

4. They shall make a showbread table with acacia wood and overlay it with pure gold. There will be gold around it and gold around the frame. They shall also make four rings of gold and put the rings on the corners, at its legs. The rings shall be close to the frame. What is the purpose of these rings?
- a. They are for design because God loved beautiful designs
- b. They are holders for the poles to bear the table
- c. For the amusement of the Israelites
- d. Serves as Moses' entrance to God's presence

5. They shall make _____ for the showbread table with pure gold and shall set the showbread on the table before God, all the time.

a. Dishes, pans, pitchers, and bowls
b. Dishes, rolling pins, spoons, and kettle
c. Dishes, cups, spoons, and pots
d. Dishes, cups, teapots, and cookies

6. They shall make a lampstand of pure gold. Its shaft, branches, bowls, ornamental knobs, and flowers shall be of one piece. What kind of work shall the lampstand be made from?
a. Molding work
b. Welding work
c. Hammered work
d. Construction work

7. This lampstand shall have _____ branches on its sides.
a. Three
b. Four
c. Five
d. Six

8. God gave Moses the number of curtains he shall use in making the Tabernacle. How many curtains shall he make it with?
a. Eleven
b. Ten
c. Nine
d. Eight

9. They shall use fine woven linen with artistic designs of cherubim to weave them. How many linens shall they use?
a. One
b. Two
c. Three
d. Four

10. They shall use fine woven linens to make the designs for the cherubim. The colors shall be blue, yellow, and red. Is it true or false?

Mountain!

Moses is still on top of the mountain, receiving instructions from God.

Quiz 44
Read Exodus 26:2-8.

God gave Moses the length of each curtain. What is the length?
a. Twenty-eight
b. Thirty-eight
c. Forty-eight
d. Fifty-eight

2. The width of the curtains was also given. What is the width of each curtain?
a. One cubit
b. Two cubits
c. Three cubits
d. Four cubits

3. They shall connect the curtains to one another. How many are there in total?
a. Three
b. Four
c. Five six
d. Six

4. They shall make loops of purple yarn on the edges of the curtains and the out edge. Is that true or false?

5. How many loops shall each curtain have?
a. Forty
b. Fifty
c. Sixty
d. Seventy

6. The color of the loops was to be _____.
a. Blue

b. Scarlet
c. Gold
d. Purple

7. They shall make a curtain of _____ over the tabernacle.
These curtains shall act as a tent over the tabernacle.
a. Goat hair
b. Sheep hair
c. Dove feathers
d. Chicken feathers

8. How many goats' hair curtains shall they make?
a. Eleven
b. Ten
c. Thirteen
d. Fourteen

9. What is the length of each goat's hair curtain?
a. Twenty cubits
b. Thirty cubits
c. Forty cubits
d. Fifty cubits

10. What is the width of each goat's hair curtain?
a. Four cubits
b. Five cubits
c. Six cubits
d. Seven cubits

Descriptions for curtains.

Quiz 45
Read Exodus 26:9-37; 27:1.

1.When the Children of Israel finished building the tabernacle, God's glory descended upon the tabernacle, and Moses could not enter because the cloud of glory filled the tabernacle. Years later, a similar incident happened when someone built a temple. Who built the temple, and who could not go into the temple?

2. They shall make five curtains by themselves and six curtains by themselves. They shall double the sixth curtain at the forefront of the tent. Again, they shall make fifty loops on each curtain. These loops will be _____.
a. Gold
b. Blue
c. Bronze
d. Purple

3. They shall use _____ to make a covering for the tent.
a. Goat skins
b. Ram skins
c. Sheepskins
d. Beef skins

4. They shall dye the ram skins scarlet. Is that true or false?

5. There shall be a covering of _____ above the ram skins.
a. Sheep skins
b. Goat skins

c. Badger skins
d. Beef skins

6. They shall make boards standing upright from _____.
a. Acacia wood
b. Metals welded together
c. Lumber wood
d. Palm tree wood

7. In total, how many boards shall they make for the south and north sides of the tabernacle?
a. Ten
b. Twenty
c. Thirty
d. Forty

8. How will they place the boards?
a. Ten each on the north, south, east, and west
b. Twenty on the south and twenty on the north
c. Twenty on the west and twenty on the east
d. All on the east to block the rising sun

9. Using acacia wood, they shall make a _____ altar for the burnt offerings.
a. Square
b. Rectangular
c. Triangular
d. Tripe zone

10. The height of the altar shall be two cubits. Is that true or false

Moses is still on the mountain.

Circle anything mentioned in Designing the Tabernacle.

A veil

A screen for the door of the Tabernacle

Bars of Acacia Wood

Board of Acacia Wood

Covering of ram skins

Quiz 46
Read Exodus 27:2-21; 28:1-8.

They shall make four horns for the altar, and the horns shall be one piece with it. They shall also overlay it with _____.
   a. Gold
   b. Bronze
   c. Silver
   d. Diamond

2. They shall make pans for the altar _____.
a. To place the animals in
b. To receive its ashes
c. To make it look unique
d. To receive the blood

3. The pans that will receive the altar's ashes - the basins, firepans, forks, and all the altar's utensils shall be overlaid with _____.
   a. Gold
   b. Bronze
   c. Silver
   d. Diamond

4. For the care of the lampstand, the Children of Israel shall bring pure pressed oil for the light, which will cause the lamp to burn continually. What kind of oil?
   a. Canola
   b. Sunflower
   c. Peanut
   d. Olive

5. _____ shall tend to the lampstand from evening until morning.

a. Abihu and his sons
b. Nadab and his sons
c. Hur and his sons
d. Aaron and his sons

6. God chose _____ to be the first priests for Himself.
a. Aaron and his sons
b. Nadab and his sons
c. Abihu and his sons
d. Hur and his sons

7. Moses shall make holy garments for Aaron. The garments are for glory and beauty. Is that true or false?

8. Moses shall speak to all gifted artisans, that they may make Aaron's and his sons' garments, to consecrate them so they may minister before the Lord as priests. The garments shall be a breastplate, an ephod, a robe, a skillfully woven tunic, a turban, and a sash. Meanwhile, God had filled all the gifted artisans with _____.
a. The spirit of sowing
b. The spirit of reverence
c. The spirit of wisdom
d. The spirit of excellence

9. They shall make the ephod with gold, blue, purple, scarlet thread, and fine linen. It shall have two shoulder straps joined at the edge. They shall make the ephod _____.
a. Artistically
b. Any old way
c. Carelessly
d. Joined any way the designer wanted

10. Moses shall take two onyx stones and ask the engravers to engrave names on them. Whose names shall they engrave on the stones?
a. The names of Aaron and his son
b. The names of the Children of Israel (Jacob)
c. The names of the artistic designers and the engravers
d. The names of Moses and his family

God Cares About Our Outside and Inside Appearance!

We found out that God chose Aaron and his four sons to be the first priests of Israel. They did not make their garments anyhow. They made them for glory and beauty. I am thinking here that God wants us to dress to give glory to Him, and He also wants us to dress beautifully. Well, I have to inspect my clothes to know if they give glory to God when I wear them. Do they look beautiful? What about you? Will you do that too?

I am done checking through all my clothes. I will now check through the inside of my heart. Beauty is not just the outside, you know. Peter said in 1 Peter 3:3-4, "Do not let your adornment be merely outward—arranging the hair, wearing gold, or putting on fine apparel—rather let it be the hidden person of the heart, with the incorruptible beauty of a gentle and quiet spirit, which is very precious in the sight of God." Wow! There is someone hiding inside our hearts. That person is the Spirit of God living inside of us. We take Him wherever we go. This hidden man doesn't die. I will try everything to make sure I take care of this man by studying the Word of God, praying, praising God, etc. I hope you will too.

Quiz 47
Read Exodus 28:9-43; 29:1-14.

1.Moses shall take two onyx stones and engrave the names of the Children of Israel on them. Six names shall be on one stone and six on the other. How shall these names be written?

    a. From youngest to oldest

    b. From oldest to youngest

    c. Leah's sons on one stone, while Rachel and Jacob's two concubines on the other

    d. No instruction was given

2. As a memorial, Moses shall bear the engraved names on his shoulder before the Lord. Is that true or false?

3. What color shall they use to make the priestly garment?

a. Red

b. Scarlet

c. Gold

d. Blue

4. They shall make a plate of pure gold, engraved with

_____.

    a. Holiness to the Lord.

    b. We are all cleansed.

    c. Praise be to the Lord.

    d. Our God is good.

5. To consecrate Aaron and his sons as priests, Moses shall take a young bull and two rams without blemish, unleavened bread, unleavened cake mixed with oil, and unleavened wafers anointed with oil. Moses shall use _____ flour to make these baked things.

    a. Wheat

b. Rice
c. Cassava
d. Corn

6. There was a cloud on top of the tabernacle of meeting. When it lifted, the Children of Israel moved and when it stayed, they will camp. What does the cloud symbolize?

7. Moses was to bring Aaron and his sons to the door of the tabernacle, and Moses was to _____.
a. Wash them with oil.
b. Wash them with wheat flour.
c. Wash them with the bull and two rams' blood.
d. Wash them with water.

8. Moses shall anoint Aaron and his sons as priests for Israel, and the priesthood shall be theirs for how long?
a. Perpetual statute
b. Until they arrive in Canaan
c. Until Aaron dies
d. Until they find another family to replace them

9. Moses shall bring the bull to the door of the tabernacle of meeting. Aaron and his sons shall do something to it while Moses kills it before the Lord. What will Aaron and his sons do to the bull?
a. They shall rub their hands on it.
b. They shall tie it down for Moses to kill.
c. They shall bring the slaughtering knife for Moses.
d. They shall put their hand on top of its heads as Moses kills it.

10. What is the name of the offering they used the bull for?
a. A sacrifice offering
b. A burnt offering
c. A sin-offering

d. A thanksgiving offering

Forgiven Forever!

Did you notice that Aaron and his sons had to place their hands on the bull for a sin offering before they killed it? That placing of hands on the bull, which became a standard for a sin offering, symbolized the transference of their sins to the bull. The Bible says the wages of sin is death. Men were supposed to die for their sins, but God has been merciful, even in the Old Testament, that He did not allow His creation to just die. Instead, He provided a means of forgiving their sins. When they lay their hands on the animal, the animal takes their sins, then it had to die for human sins. That was the shadow of what Jesus finally did for us. When He died for our sins, all the sins we will ever commit were placed on Him. That means God is not imputing (recording) sins for us (2 Corinthians 5:19). Praise the name of the Lord!

Circle anything that is part of the Priestly Garment.

A robe   A neck lace

A coat   Tunic

A sword   A breastplate

Sash   A rod

Turban   A sandal

A plate of pure gold

Quiz 48
Read Exodus 29:15-33

They used the first ram for a _ _ _ _ _ offering.
    a. Burnt
    b. Thanksgiving
    c. Sacrifice
    d. Sin

2. They described the burnt offering as having a sweet aroma. Is that true or false?

3. Moses will kill the second ram as Aaron and his sons put their hands on it. He shall use some blood from the ram to touch Aaron and his sons' right ear and right big toe, and he shall also sprinkle some blood on them. This ram is called _ _ _ _ _ _ _ _.
    a. A ram of forgiveness
    b. A ram of blessing
    c. A ram of the chosen
    d. A ram of consecration

4. Moses shall take the intestines of the ram and its fats, together with one loaf of bread, one cake made with oil, and one wafer from the basket of the unleavened bread before the Lord. He shall put all these in the hands of Aaron and his sons. Then, Moses shall wave them before the Lord. This offering is called
_ _ _ _ _ _ _.
    a. A burnt offering
    b. A sin-offering
    c. A blessing offering
    d. A wave offering

5. Moses shall take the things he placed on Aaron and his sons' hands back and then use them for _ _ _ _ _ _ _.

a. A burnt offering
b. A sin-offering
c. A blessing offering
d. A sacrifice offering

6. There is an offering Moses shall make by using the breast of the ram of consecration. What is the name of that offering?
a. A burnt offering
b. A sin-offering
c. A wave offering
d. A blessing offering

7. When Aaron dies, they shall transfer his holy garment to
_____.
a. The sons of Hur
b. The sons of Dothan
c. The sons of Korah
d. Aaron's sons

8. Aaron's son, who shall replace him in his priestly duties, shall put his garments on for three days. Is that true or false?

9. Moses shall take the ram of consecration, boil its flesh in the holy place, and some people shall eat it with the bread in the basket by the door of the Tabernacle of Meeting. Who are those people that shall eat the ram of consecration?
a. Aaron and his sons
b. The elders of the children of Israel
c. The congregation
d. The widows

10. Aaron and his sons shall eat the boiled ram of the consecration with the bread in the basket by the door of the tabernacle of meeting. There is a reason they shall eat this meal. What is the reason?
a. To reward them for their hard work
b. To encourage them for all they had done
c. To consecrate and sanctify them
d. To make them be like Moses

Separated Unto God!

This place is talking about how Aaron and his sons, being the first priest of Israel, are being separated unto the Lord for the work He had called them to do. Moses will make a burnt offering, which is also called a sweet aroma. A burnt offering is burnt unto the Lord on an altar. There is also a wave offering.

Just as Aaron and his sons lived a separate life in their time, we, as God's chosen ones, are to live a separate life today (2 Corinthians 6:16-18).

Quiz 49
Read Exodus 29:33-46; 30:1-7.

1.What shall happen to the remains of the ram of the consecration and the bread in the morning?
   a. They shall throw them to the birds of the air.
   b. They shall be burned with fire.
   c. They shall bury them.
   d. They shall be given in pieces to each firstborn of the Levites.

2. Moses shall consecrate Aaron and his sons for _____.
   a. Eight days
   b. Seven days
   c. Six days
   d. Five days

3. Moses shall make an offering, using a bull, every day of the seven days of the consecration. What kind of offering is it?
   a. Heave offering
   b. Burnt offering
   c. Sin offering
   d. Weave offering

4. For seven days, Moses shall make a sin offering for Aaron and his sons, using a bull, and seven days Moses shall make an atonement for the altar and sanctify it. After those seven days of atonement for the altar, the altar shall be most holy. From that day forward, before someone can touch that altar, the person must be _____.
   a. Holy
   b. A widower
   c. A widow
   d. An elder

5. Throughout Moses' generation, he was to offer a daily offering. How many times a day?
a. Once
b. Twice
c. Thrice
d. Four times

6. Moses was to offer two offerings daily. God told him to use lambs of the second year for the offerings. Is it true or false?

7. Moses shall offer two lambs of the first year, one in the morning and the other in the evening. He shall offer this lamb along with a _____.
a. Burnt and sin-offering
b. Grain and drink offering
c. Heave and wave offering
d. Wave and sin offering

8. Moses shall make an incense altar. Its length and width shall be one cubit, and its height shall be how many cubits?
a. One
b. Two
c. Three
d. Four

9. The height of the incense altar shall be two cubits, and its horns shall be of one piece with it. Also, Moses shall overlay its sides, top, and horns with _____.
a. Gold
b. Silver
c. Bronze
d. Diamond

10. Who shall burn incense on this altar?
a. Moses
b. Aaron
c. Aaron's sons take turns, starting from the oldest
d. The elders of Israel, starting from the oldest

Obey God's Command!

Aaron shall burn incense on this incense altar, morning and evening, every day of his life. What if he forgets? What if he doesn't feel like burning the incense? What if someone offends him and he is angry? You see..., a command is a command. God cannot ask us to do something He knows we cannot do. Once He asks us to do something, we have to obey, whether we feel like doing it (We will see how Aaron will act when tragedy struck his family in a forthcoming series—Leviticus). Even when someone looks down on us, thinks we are not smart enough, or we lose our game, etc. We have to obey God's Word at all times. For example, His word said, "Rejoice in the Lord always. Again I will say, rejoice! (Philippians 4:4). Oh, one more. 1 Thessalonians 5:16-18 says, "Rejoice always, pray without ceasing, in everything give thanks; for this is the will of God in Christ Jesus for you." He said we should rejoice always. What? Even when I lose my game? Even when my friend did not invite me to a birthday party? Yes! You are to rejoice. There in the verse, it also says we should pray without ceasing (not giving up). When you are praying about something, you should not stop praying about it until you see the answer. You prayed about it today, tomorrow, two weeks later, and so on. You will pray until you see the answer. That is praying without ceasing. Last, when you hit your head, feel sad, or lose your game, thank God. It's not the end of the world. You thank and pray that He should help you be better. What do you think? Can you do that?

Quiz 50
Read Exodus 30:7-25.

1.Aaron shall burn incense on the altar _ _ _ _ times a day?
 a. five
 b. Two
 c. Three
 d. Four

2. The priest shall wear a turban of fine linen, short trousers of fine woven linen, a sash of linen, etc. There is a reason they were to wear linen, and it is not given to us in Exodus, but can be found in Ezekiel 44:18. Why is the priest required to wear linen?

3. They shall not offer strange incense, grain offerings, or _ _ _ _ _ on the incense altar.
 a. Burnt offerings
 b. Sin-offerings
 c. Drink offerings
 d. Wave offerings

4. Aaron shall make an atonement upon the horns of the incense altar once a year. Is that true or false?

5. All the Children of Israel that were counted during a census were to give a ransom for themselves unto the Lord. This they must do to avoid _ _ _ _ _ _.
 a. Sinning
 b. Slavery

c. Being plagued

d. Suffering

6. How old shall an Israelite male be before he is qualified to be counted during their census?

a. Sixteen years

b. Seventeen years

c. Nineteen years

d. Twenty years

7. Moses shall make a laver of bronze and put it between the Tabernacle of Meeting and the altar. What shall be placed in it?

a. Flour

b. Water

c. Only unleavened bread

d. Grains

8. _____ shall use the water inside the bronze laver to wash their hands and feet when they go into the tabernacle to do their duties.

a. Aaron and his sons

b. All the elders of the Children of Israel

c. All the males twenty years of age

d. Everyone that goes into the tabernacle

9. Aaron and his sons shall wash their hands and feet when they go into the Tabernacle of Meeting or come near the altar to minister burnt offerings before the Lord. What will happen if they don't?

a. They will be taken out of the priesthood.

b. They will cause a plague on the people.

c. They will become leprous.

d. They will die.

10. Moses shall use quality spices, myrrh, cinnamon, sweet-smelling cane, cassia, and a hin of olive oil to make _____.

a. Dough

b. Bread

c. Unleavened cake

d. Holy anointing oil

Do Only What God Ask You to Do!

Here, we saw the command from the Lord through Moses that they "shall not offer strange incense on it, or a burnt offering, or a grain offering; nor shall they pour a drink offering on it" (Exodus 30:9). You can find out what happened when some people disobey this rule in the next series—Leviticus.

Quiz 51
Read Exodus 30:26-38; 31:1-18.

1.Moses shall use the holy anointing oil to anoint the tabernacle and everything in it. He shall also use it to anoint Aaron and his sons, to consecrate them as ministers to the Lord and priests. The Israelites shall not make any oil composition like the holy anointing oil. If anyone disobeyed and made any oil like it, that person would be _____.
   a. Banished
   b. Burned with fire
   c. Cut off from his people
   d. Stoned

2. God gave Moses a combination of items to be used as incense, and no one shall make that composition to smell it because something shall happen to the person who made it. What shall happen to that person?
   a. He shall be cut off.
   b. He shall be banished.
   c. He shall be burnt.
   d. He shall be stoned.

3. Hur had a grandson whom God filled with His Spirit. What is this man's name?
   a. Aholiab
   b. Ahisamach
   c. Phinehas
   d. Bezalel

4. Who is the direct father of Bezalel?
   a. Aholiab
   b. Ahisamach
   c. Uri

d. Phinehas

5. Bezalel, Uri, and Hur are from which tribe in Israel?
a. Rueben
b. Levi
c. Judah
d. Simeon

6. God filled Bezalel with His Spirit in understanding, wisdom, knowledge, and all manner of craft. Which of those qualities was mentioned first?
a. Calmness
b. Wisdom
c. Building
d. Drawing

7. God appointed Bezalel and the son of Ahisamach in the artisans' things. What is the name of Ahisamach's son?
a. Aholiab
b. Uri
c. Phinehas
d. Rueben

8. Aholiab is from which tribe in Israel?
a. Rueben
b. Levi
c. Simeon
d. Dan

9. They shall kill a person who profanes the Sabbath. Is that true or false?

10. When God finished speaking to Moses on Mount Sinai, He gave him _____.
a. Two tablets of the Testimony
b. Two tablets of Punishments
c. Two tablets of Medication
d. Two tablets of Honor

The Name of Jesus!

God filled Bezalel and Aholiab with His Spirit, in wisdom, in understanding, in knowledge, and in all manner of workmanship (Exodus 31:3). Hmm..., what do you think? First, God filled them with His Spirit. If you are born again, you are filled with God's Spirit, too. Do you think you lack wisdom, and understanding in math, science, etc? Do you think you need more skills in your favorite sport? Talk to God! Tell Him to show you or teach you what you want to be good at. He is very willing to give it to you. You see..., in Mathew 5:7:7-8, Jesus said you should, "Ask, and it will be given to you; seek, and you will find; knock, and it will be opened to you. For everyone who asks receives, and he who seeks finds, and to him who knocks it will be opened." He said "everyone" who asks, seeks, knocks. That includes you too. The opposite of it is that, if you don't ask, you won't be given. If you don't seek, you won't find, and if you don't knock, the door won't be open to you. Now, are you ready to ask, my friend? Wait, wait, wait, I almost forgot. Do not just say something like—Lord, I need to improve my baseball catching skill, amen. No, no, no! You have to give thanks. Remember what we said earlier? "In everything, give thanks". Again, you have to add the name of Jesus to it. So, you would pray something like–Lord, thank you for giving me life. Please help me improve my baseball-catching skills. Thank you for answering me. In Jesus' name. Amen!

Do you know why you have to ask in the name of Jesus? Well, that was His command to us. You know whether we feel good, when God says we should do something, we have to do it, right? Jesus said we should ask in His name. He gave us the guarantee that anything we ask using His name, He will do it. We have to ask according to His will, though. When He answers our prayer, His Father, God, who is now our Father, will be glorified (John 14:13-14).

Quiz 52
Read Exodus 31:18 32:1-11.

What was written on the tablets?
    a. Poems
    b. Praises unto God
    c. Commandments
    d. Random things

2. Who wrote on the tablets?
    a. Moses
    b. Joshua
    c. God
    d. Angel

3. God wrote on the tablets with His spoken Words. Is that true or false?

4. Today, in churches, people give an offering. Who started the giving of an offering?

5. When the people waited for Moses and did not return as they expected, the Israelites asked _ _ _ _ _ _ to make gods for them.
    a. Hur
    b. Eleazer
    c. Abihu
    d. Aaron

6. When the people asked Aaron to make gods for them, he asked for their _____.
a. Diamond earrings
b. Golden earrings
c. Bronze and golden earrings
d. All the above

7. As he had asked, the people brought their golden earrings to Aaron, and he used them to make _____.
a. A head
b. A round stone
c. A crocodile
d. A calf

8. When he made the calf, he also built an altar. Is that true or false?

9. Aaron proclaimed to the people that tomorrow is a feast for the Lord, and when they rose in the morning, they _____.
a. Offered a sin offering
b. Offered a wave offering
c. Offered a drink offering
d. Offered a burnt offering

10. The Lord was angry with the Israelites and wanted to wipe them out from the earth and raise a nation from Moses, but Moses_____.
a. Slapped himself to appease God for the Israelites
b. Pleaded with God for the Israelites
c. Asked God to give them a second chance to come back to Him.
d. Told God he would handle them in his way

Broken Promise!

In quiz 38, we talked about Aaron, his four sons, and seventy elders of Israel who practically saw the glory at the feet of God. They describe how it looks. God had called Moses up the mountain, leaving the congregation of Israel under the care of Aaron and Hur. These people who had seen God's glory remarkably could not still their people to stop asking Aaron to make them a god. Now they have broken the commitment they made to the Lord, "All that the Lord had said, we will do?" The instruction was for them to wait, and they couldn't.

Quiz 53
Read Exodus 32:12-35; 33:1-7.

When Moses was pleading with the Lord for the Israelites, he asked God to remember _____.
- a. The Egyptians
- b. The Canaanites
- c. The philistines
- d. Abraham, Isaac, and Jacob

2. Who was waiting for Moses on top of the mountain?
- a. Hur
- b. Aaron
- c. Joshua
- d. Abihu

3. When Moses saw the people in the worship of the golden calf, he did something to the tablets in his hand. What did he do to them?
- a. He broke them at the foot of the mountain as he cast them down.
- b. He took them back to the top of the mountain.
- c. He kept them safe at the foot of the mountain.
- d. He buried them at the foot of the mountain.

4. Moses took the calf, burned it to powder, scattered it on the water, and made the Israelites _____.
- a. Swim in it to their shame
- b. Drink from it
- c. Made the people repent
- d. Bathe in it

5. Moses stood at the camp entrance, and he told the Israelites that whoever was on the Lord's side should come to him. Some

people from the twelve tribes of Israel came to him. What tribe were those people from?

a. Rueben
b. Judah
c. Simeon
d. Levi

6. Moses told the Levites to kill their neighbors because of the worship of the golden calf, and they did according to what Moses had said. That day, _____ men died?

a. About two thousand
b. About three thousand
c. About four thousand
d. About five thousand

7. The following day, Moses went back to the Lord and told Him that the people had sinned and that He should forgive their sin, but if He would not, he asked God to _____.

a. Remove him from being their leader.
b. Blot him out of the book He has written.
c. Remove him from being His friend.
d. Kill him and his son, instead.

8. God said something to Moses when he requested the Lord blot him out of the book He had written. What did He say to Moses?

a. Whoever has sinned against Me, I will blot him out of My book.
b. I will blot those that sinned against their families and me out of my book.
c. I will blot nobody that sinned out of my book.
d. I will do whatever I want, for I am God.

9. God asked Moses to tell the Children of Israel that they should leave Mount Horeb and move to the land He had promised them, but He would not be in their midst lest He consumed them on the way because of their stubbornness. The Lord also said the Children of Israel should _____.

a. Mourn for their wickedness
b. Take off their ornaments
c. Fast for three days

d. Put on sack clothes

10. Moses took his tent, pitched it outside the camp, far from the people, and then he called it the tent of the Lord. Is that true or false?

Take Responsibility!

We saw how Moses blamed Aaron for not restraining the Children of Israel when they came to meet him to make a god for them (Exodus 32:21, 25). Leaders have a lot to carry. If you have a younger sibling, you might have been yelled at for a crime committed by your younger one. That is because your parents want you to look after your younger siblings. They want you to make sure they didn't do what was wrong under your watch. In the first series of this book—Genesis, we talked about how the Lord asked Abraham why Sarah laughed when He could have asked Sarah herself. Responsibility. We have to take responsibility for those under our care. If you are the noise maker in class, I want you to know that you are giving your teacher a lot of stress, because they are doing everything they can to make sure everyone learns. Your noise-making might stop your classmates from learning the way they ought, and your teacher will give an account if not to anyone..., to themselves if they did the right thing. Did I just say, 'give an account'? Yes. Your parents will give an account to God on your behalf, so do everything to make sure you follow their instructions. I believe they want everything to be well with you. Otherwise, they won't bother to buy this book. They are doing their part, now you should do yours.

Quiz 54
Read Exodus 33:8-18.

Whenever Moses is going to the Tabernacle of Meeting, the people would _____.
    a. Wave bye-bye to him.
    b. Hide in their tents because they were ashamed of worshipping the golden calf.
    c. Stand in front of their tents and watch Moses until he enters the tabernacle.
    d. Be singing a sorrowful song so God could forgive them.

2. Whenever Moses entered the Tabernacle of Meeting, _____.
    a. A pillar of fire would appear at the door of the tabernacle, and the Lord talked with Moses.
    b. A pillar of cloud descended and stood at the door of the tabernacle, and the Lord talked with Moses.
    c. A pillar of fire and cloud both appeared and stood at the door of the tabernacle as the Lord talked with Moses.
    d. There was smoke on top of the tabernacle as the Lord talked with Moses.

3. Whenever Moses went into the Tabernacle of Meeting, the pillar of cloud would descend as the Lord talked with Moses, and when the people saw the pillar of cloud, they would _____.
    a. Weep for joy because the Lord had not left them.
    b. Worship each man in his tent.
    c. Celebrate Jehovah, the Lord of Hosts.
    d. Dance for joy.

4. Each time Moses went to the Tabernacle of Meeting, the Lord spoke to him. How did He speak to Moses?
    a. He spoke to him in the shade.

b. He spoke to him from behind.

c. He spoke to him face to face, as a man speaks to his friend.

d. He spoke to him in an audible voice.

5. Moses would go to the Tabernacle of Meeting and come back to the Hebrews' camp, but Joshua always stayed back at the tabernacle. Is that true or false?

6. Joshua had a father. What was his name?

a. Nun

b. Hur

c. Ruel

d. Jethro

7. The Lord told Moses that he had found grace in His sight and that _____.

a. Moses was precious in His sight.

b. He knows him by name.

c. He is faithful to Moses.

d. He put His rod in his hand.

8. The Lord said to Moses, "I know you by name, and you have found grace in My sight." Then Moses said to the Lord that if he had found grace in His sight, the Lord should show him His way, and He should consider the nation of Israel to be _____.

a. His children

b. His name forever

c. His heritage

d. His people

9. What did Moses say to the Lord about His presence?

a. We only need Your presence when we are about to fight with our enemies.

b. Your presence is too much for us, for the people are always disobedient to You, and I don't want You to kill all of us.

c. Do not remove us from here if Your presence will not go with us.

d. Let Your presence stay behind us.

10. Moses also asked God to _____.

a. Let His grace multiply upon him.

b. Show him His glory.
c. Give him the grace to lead His people.
d. Please help them in their unbelief.

Tabernacle of Meeting!

Moses pitched a tent outside the camp of Israel. Moses will go into the tabernacle of meeting while everyone is washing. When he entered, the glory of God will descend, then God will speak to him face to face. Joshua, however, never left the tent of meeting. The name of Joshua's father was also given.

Quiz 55
Exodus 33:19-23; 34:1-35.

Moses asked God to show him His glory; then, the Lord said to Moses that He would make His goodness pass before him and He would proclaim His name to Him. He will be gracious to whom He wants to be gracious to, show compassion to whom He wants to; then He said to Moses, that _____.

a. That he cannot see His face; for no man shall see Him and live.

b. Moses can only see His hand.

c. He shall see His glory in the cloud.

d. He shall see His glory in the pillar of fire by night.

2. God told Moses that when He would pass by, He would put Moses in the rock's cleft and He would use His hand to cover Moses' face while He passed by, but Moses will see a part of Him. What part did He say Moses would see?

a. His forehead

b. His hand

c. His head

d. His back

3. The Lord wrote the Ten Commandments on two tablets from the same mountain the second time. What mountain was that, anyway?

a. Mount Horeb

b. Mount Sinai

c. Mount Israel

d. Mount Olivet

4. The Lord told Moses that He would be with the Israelites and do marvelous things among them. He would drive away their enemies. He told Moses they should not make covenants with the

inhabitants of the land where they were going. Why did God ask the Israelites not to make covenants with the people of the land they were going to?
a. So they can be different
b. Lest the people war with them
c. Lest the inhabitants be snares in their midst
d. Lest they marry their girls

5. God told Moses they should break down the people's altars they would live with. He told them they should not worship their gods because God is a _____.
a. Good God
b. Righteous God
c. Jealous God
d. Merciful God

6. God told Moses, they shall work for six days, and on the seventh day, they shall rest _____.
a. During plowing season
b. During harvest season
c. Throughout the entire year, even during the plowing and harvest seasons
d. During wheat season

7. Moses spent several days on the mountain when God gave him the second set of Ten Commandments. How many days did he stay?
a. Forty days
b. Forty-one days
c. Forty-three days
d. Forty-four days

8 When Moses came down from the mountain, the people saw his face _____.
a. Was dark
b. Was pilled
c. Shone
d. Was speckled

9. When the Hebrews saw Moses' face shining, they celebrated him. Is that true or false?

10. Moses' face shone when he came from the top of the mountain, so he _ _ _ _ _ whenever he was among the people.
   a. Stayed in the tent
   b. Stayed in the Tabernacle of Meeting
   c. Veiled himself
   d. Stayed behind Joshua

Re-Giving of the Ten Commandment!

Remember that the Feast of Unleavened Bread that is mentioned in verse eighteen is the same as the Passover Feast.

Here is the re-giving of the Ten Commandments. Do you remember Moses broke the first one? Now he went back to receive the second one. Moses was there on top of the mountain for another forty days. He was there for the first time for forty days, too. Altogether, how many days did Moses stay on top of the mountain? Yeah! Eighty days. This time, though, the Israelites did not ask Aaron to make a god for them.

Quiz 56
Read Exodus 35:2; 39:42-43; 40.

1.A person was to be _____ if they worked on the Sabbath.
   a. Killed
   b. Banished
   c. Sold
   d. Flogged

2. In Exodus 40:20, Moses put the testimony into the ark, inserted the poles through the ark's ring, and put the mercy seat on top of the ark. What is being referred to as the testimony here?

3. Moses told the people that the Lord had said they should bring gifts for building the tabernacle and making the priesthood garments. What people obeyed?
   a. People whose heart was stirred and those whose spirit was willing
   b. All the people that have the requirements the Lord had given to Moses
   c. All those who were from Moses' family
   d. All the elders

4. Some people brought onyx stones for the ephod and breast-plate. Who were these people?
   a. The women
   b. The men
   c. The older people
   d. The rulers

5. The Children of Israel brought more than was needed because every morning, the people brought _____.
   a. A freewill offering
   b. Food for the workers
   c. Clothing for the workers
   d. Bread for the workers

6. When Moses looked at all that the people had done in building the tabernacle and everything the Lord had commanded him, he saw everything was done as God had told him. What did Moses do?
   a. He blessed the Lord.
   b. He blessed the people.
   c. He praised the Lord.
   d. He praised the people.

7. The Lord told Moses to set up the tabernacle _____.
   a. On the first day of the first month.
   b. On the second day of the first month.
   c. On the third day of the first month.
   d. On the fourth day of the first month.

8. The tabernacle was raised in the ____ year on the first day of the month.
   a. First
   b. Second
   c. Third
   d. Fourth

9. When the tabernacle was finished, _____.
   a. The glory of the Lord filled it.
   b. The tabernacle was red.
   c. The tabernacle was grey.
   d. The tabernacle was quaking.

10. Moses could not do something because the glory of the Lord filled the tabernacle. What was Moses not able to do?
    a. He could not pray.
    b. He was unable to go in and worship.
    c. He was not able to go into the tabernacle.

d. He was not able to offer a sin offering.

11. The cloud was on top of the tabernacle as the Israelites journeyed for the next 38 years. They will move if the cloud is taken up, and they will stay if the cloud stayed. Is that true or false?

12. Moses brought the ark into the tabernacle, set up a covering veil, and covered the testimony's ark (Exodus 40:21). What does the veil symbolize?

Favor!

I skipped chapters 36-39 because almost everything is a repetition of what we have done. We have followed how God gave Moses the design of the tabernacle and the ornaments. The chapters I jumped are using the instructions to build the tabernacle and its ornaments.

Now we saw the fire element. This time, the fire never went off until the Children of Israel arrived at their destination. Every night, they would see the fire on top of the tabernacle. What a wonderful God we serve!

I need a favor from you, though. I need you to count each of your elements and send the numbers to me. You can refer back to when the plagues started, so I can know. I will wait to receive a message from you. You can reach me at onlyonelifstory.com.

Conclusion

First, thank you for purchasing this Exodus-focused Bible quiz. I advise you to please take some time to go through it again. I know you could have picked any other book to read, but you chose this one, and for that, I am incredibly grateful.

I would love to see many other children taught God's truths in their homes. If I was valuable to you in that way, please leave an honest review on Amazon or your bookstore, and it will encourage other parents to teach their children about God—with my help.

I also encourage you to check out my Amazon store for more of my books.

Answer Keys

Quiz 1

    1. B. Pharaoh

    2. C. They would join forces with their enemies and war against them (Exodus 1:10).

    3. C. They set up taskmasters over them to afflict them with their burden (Exodus 1:11).

    4. A. Supply cities, Pithom and Raamses (Exodus 1:11)

    5. D. He asked them to kill all the boy babies (Exodus 1:16).

    6. True (Exodus 1:15)

    7. A. Shiphrah and Puah (Exodus 1:15)

    8. Abram (Genesis 14:13)

    9. D. Because they feared God (Exodus 1:17)

    10. They said the Israelite women were not like the Egyptian women because they were lively and gave birth before they could get there (Genesis 1:19).

Quiz 2

    1. D. He provided households for them (Exodus 1:21).

    2. C. He asked them to throw every male baby into the river (Exodus 1:22).

    3. D. Jochebed (Exodus 6:20)

    4. D. Amram (Exodus 6:20)

5. False. They both came from the tribe of Levi (Exodus 2:1)

6. Jacob (Genesis 32:28)

7. B. She knew the child was beautiful (Exodus 2:2).

8. B. Three months (Exodus 2:2)

9. False. Jochebed and Amram's daughter's name was Miriam

10. A. Aaron

Quiz 3

1. True (Exodus 2:3)

2. A. She daubed it with asphalt and pitch (Exodus 2:3)

3. D. In the reeds (Exodus 2:3)

4. C. What would happen to her baby brother (Exodus 2:4)

5. B. The daughter of Pharaoh (Exodus 2:5)

6. C. She came to bathe (Exodus 2:5)

7. False. She came with her maidens (Exodus 2:5)

8. D. He was crying (Exodus 2:6)

9. C. Should I find a Hebrew woman to nurse him for you? (Exodus 2:7)

10. D. She went to call the baby's mom, who was also her mom (Exodus 2:8)

Quiz 4

1. A. Wages (Exodus 2:9)

2. D. Moses (Exodus 2:10)

3. It was paid to Jochebed to take care of her son, Moses (Exodus 2:9).

4. B. He killed the Egyptian person and buried him in the

sand (Exodus 2:12).

5. D. He saw two Israelites fighting (Exodus 2:13).

6. C. Who made you a prince and a judge? Do you want to kill me the way you killed the Egyptian the other day? (Exodus 2:14)

7. C. Forty years

8. A. Midian (Exodus 2:15)

9. False. He sat by a well (Exodus 2:15).

10. C. Seven (Exodus 2:16)

Quiz 5
1. B. Stood up for the seven sisters, helped them, and then watered their flock (Exodus 2:17)

2. False. The priest of Midian's name was Reuel (Exodus 2:18).

3. B. That he might eat bread (Exodus 2:20)

4. C. Zipporah (Exodus 2:21)

5. Melchizedek

6. A. Two

False. Their first son's name was Gershom (Exodus 2:22)
1. B. Stranger here (Exodus 2:22)

2. A. Eliezer (Exodus 18:4)

3. B. He died (Exodus 2:23).

Quiz 6
1. A. His covenant with Abraham, Isaac, and Jacob (Exodus 2:24)

2. True (Exodus 3:1)

3. C. His father-in-law, Reuel's sheep (Exodus 3:1)

4. B. Jethro (Exodus 3:1)

5. A. Horeb (Exodus 3:1)

6. A. The Mountain of God (Exodus 3:1)

7. False. He appeared to him in a flame of fire (Exodus 3:2)

8. C. In a bush (Exodus 3:2)

9. D. Do not draw near this place. Take off your sandals from your feet, for the place you are standing on is holy ground (Exodus 3:5).

10. An abomination to the Egyptian

Quiz 7

1. A. He introduced Himself to Moses (Exodus 3:6).

2. B. He wants to bring them to the land He had promised their fathers–the land flowing with milk and honey (Exodus 3:8).

3. C. I have seen how Pharaoh is oppressing My children, and I want to send you to him, and you will bring My people, the Children of Israel, out of Egypt (Exodus 3:9).

4. B. You shall serve me on this mountain when you have brought Israel out of Egypt (Exodus 3:12).

5. C. I AM Who I Am (Exodus 3:14)

6. B. Three days (Exodus 3:18)

7. A. Articles of silver, articles of gold, and clothing Exodus 3:22

8. D. It changed to a snake/serpent (Exodus 4:3).

9. False. God asked Moses to pick the snake by the tail (Exodus 4:4)

10. D. His hand became leprous, like snow (Exodus 4:6).

Quiz 8

1. B. Blood (Exodus 4:9)

2. Joseph, Jesus, and Herod

3. C. I am not a good speaker (Exodus 4:10).

4. D. His mouth and teach him what to say (Exodus 4:12)

5. B. His brother, Aaron (Exodus 4:14)

6. A. As god (Exodus 4:16)

7. B. Four times (Exodus 3:11; 3:13; 4:1, and 4:10)

8. C. They were dead (Exodus 4:19).

9. B. His wife and two sons (Exodus 4:20)

10. False. Moses used a donkey (Exodus 4:20)

Quiz 9

1. C. The rod of God (Exodus 4:20)

2. A. Israel is His son, His firstborn (Exodus 4:22)

3. True (Exodus 4:23)

4. D. Took a sharp stone and cut off the foreskin of her son and cast it at Moses' feet (Exodus 4:25).

5. Yes, the Lord wanted to kill Moses because he did not keep the commandment the Lord gave to Abraham about circumcising every male child. Anyone who did not obey the circumcision law was to be killed (cut off) (Genesis 17:19-14). Moses did not obey this law because either one, or his two sons, wasn't circumcised. Zipporah saved the day by circumcising their son(s) with a sharp stone.

6. D. All the signs the Lord had shown him (Exodus 4:30)

7. C. Believed, bowed their heads, and worshipped (Exodus 4:31)

8. C. Straw (Exodus 5:7)

9. A. You are idle! That is why you have asked me to release you so that you can offer your sacrifice to the Lord (Exodus 5:17).

10. A. God Almighty (Exodus 6:2)

Quiz 10

1. A. Lord (Exodus 6:3)

2. False. Aaron had four sons (Exodus 6:23)

3. B. Nadab, Abihu, Eleazer, and Ithamar (Exodus 6:23)

4. C. Phinehas (Exodus 6:25)

5. A. As god (Exodus 7:1)

6. C. A prophet (Exodus 7:1)

7. B. A He was eighty years old (Exodus 7:7)

8. False. Aaron was eighty-three years old (Exodus 7:7).

9. C. Aaron's rod swallowed up the magicians' snake (Exodus 7:12).

10. C. Ten

Quiz 11

1. No. God is not unjust to harden Pharaoh's heart. Stubbornness was Pharaoh's choice. In our Genesis series, we said man is like God in many ways. Man, like God, has the power to make choices. God did not create man to be a robot, so He gave man the power to choose. Not yielding to God's instruction was Pharaoh's choice. In Exodus 3:19, when God talked to Moses, He told Moses that He knew Pharaoh would not let them go. God knew this because He could see the future. He was only telling Moses what Pharaoh would do, not because He chose his fate for him. Far be it from God! He gives everyone equal rights to make their choices. In Deuteronomy 30:19, Moses told the Children of Israel that they could choose between life and death. In this same verse and chapter, Moses told them to choose life. This is how it is for us today. We can

choose to come to God through the One Way that is the Truth and the Life—Jesus (John 14:6). But people today choose to go the opposite way. Does that mean God was the one that chose the opposite way for them? No!

We all have an opportunity to choose life (everlasting life with Jesus). It's easy, and all you need to do is "... confess with your mouth the Lord Jesus and believe in your heart that God has raised Him from the dead, and you will be saved" (Romans 10:9).
2. B. Water becomes blood (Exodus 7:20)
3. B. Aaron stretched the rod of God over the waters of Egypt, the streams, rivers, ponds, and pools of water (Exodus 7:19).
1. B. Seven days (Exodus 7:25)

2. A. They dug all around the river to get water to drink (Exodus 7:24).

3. A. Frogs (Exodus 8:6)

4. True (Exodus 8:6)

5. B. Tomorrow (Exodus 8:10)

6. False, Moses told Pharaoh the frogs will stay in the river, only (Exodus 8:11)

7. C. The frogs died (Exodus 8:13).

Quiz 12
1. D. They gathered them together in heaps (Exodus 8:14)

2. A. It stank (Exodus 8:14).

3. False. Pharaoh hardened his heart (Exodus 8:15)

4. B. Lice (Exodus 8:17)

5. C. Stretch out his rod and strike the land's dust (Exodus 8:16).

6. D. They could not bring out lice (Exodus 8:18).

7. D. The lice were on both human beings and beasts (Exodus 8:18).

8. C. They said, "This is the finger of God" (Exodus 8:19).

9. A. Flies (Exodus 8:24)

Quiz 13

1. D. Only the Egyptians will receive the plague of the flies, but Goshen, where the Israelites lived, will not have swarms of flies (Exodus 8:22).

2. A. He is the Lord amid the land (Exodus 8:22).

3. B. Go and sacrifice to his God in the land (Exodus 8:25).

4. A. The Egyptians would hate their sacrifices (for they would complain to God about the Egyptians) and want to stone them (Exodus 8:26).

5. B. They would go on a three-day journey into the wilderness and sacrifice to the Lord their God (Exodus 8:27).

6. B. Do not go far away and intercede for me (Exodus 8:28).

7. A. He hardened his heart and did not keep his promise of letting them go away to sacrifice and intercede for him (Exodus 8:32).

8. False. The fifth plague was the death of livestock (Exodus 9:6).

9. D. He put a difference between the livestock of the Egyptians and that of the Israelites because it was only the Egyptians' livestock that died (Exodus 9:4).

10. C. Sent to know if the livestock of the Children of Israel had died Exodus 9:7

Quiz 14

1. D. Boils that break out in sores (Exodus 9:10)

2. D. He asked him to take a handful of ashes from a furnace and scatter it toward the heavens in the sight of Pharaoh (Exodus 9:8).

3. True (Exodus 9:9)

4. C. Man and beast (Exodus 9:10)

5. D. Hail (Exodus 9:23)

6. A. That He might show His power in him and His name may be declared in all the earth (Exodus 9:16)

7. A. Every man, beast, and herb (Exodus 9:19)

8. False. Those who were afraid of the Lord's Word removed theirs (Exodus 9:20)

9. D. Stretch out his hand toward Heaven (Exodus 9:22)

10. D. Sinned this time. The Lord is righteous, and my people and I are wicked (Exodus 9:27).

Quiz 15

1. B. Spread out his hands to the Lord (Exodus 9:29).

2. A. The flax, barley, and wheat (Exodus 9:31-32)

3. True (Exodus 9:32)

4. B. The hearing of their sons and son's sons (Exodus 10:2)

5. D. Locusts (Exodus 10:4)

6. A. The men (Exodus 10:11)

7. B. They drove them out of Pharaoh's presence (Exodus 10:11).

8. A. Stretch out his hand (rod) over the land of Egypt (Exodus 10:13).

9. False. The Lord brought an east wind on the land all day and night (Exodus 10:13).

10. B. He had sinned against the Lord their God and them. They should forgive his sin this time and entreat the Lord their God to take this death away from him only this time (Exodus 10:16-17).

Quiz 16

1. D. A strong west wind (Exodus 10:19)

2. False. The wind blew the locusts to the Red Sea (Exodus 10:19)

3. C. Darkness (Exodus 10:22)

4. B. Stretch his hand toward Heaven (Exodus 10:21).

5. B. Three days (Exodus 10:22)

6. D. He asked Moses to let their flocks and herds stay behind" (Exodus 10:24).

7. A. Go away from him and be careful not to see his face again because the day he does, he will die (Exodus 10:28)

8. D. Well-spoken, I will never see your face again (Exodus 10:29).

9. The Passover was collective salvation, but in Jesus, everyone has to appropriate the salvation of Jesus for themselves. You can't say that because my dad or mom is born again, I am born again. No, you will have to decide for yourself which is the difference. It is one by one to Jesus for salvation. If you are not saved, you can do it right now. God makes it easy to be born again–refer to quiz 11 question 1 answer for how to be born again.

10. C. Death of the Egyptian's firstborn (Exodus12:29)

Quiz 17

1. D. Favor (Exodus 11:3)

2. False. The Lord said, about midnight (Exodus 11:4)

3. C. The firstborn of both humans and animals (Exodus 11:5)

4. D. In the sight of Pharaoh's servants and the people (Exodus 11:3)

5. A. The month of Abib (Exodus 23:15)

6. C. On the tenth of the month (Exodus 12:3)

7. B. A lamb (Exodus 12:3)

8. D. If a family is too small, that family and his neighbor should take a lamb according to each man's needs (Exodus 12:4).

9. A. Without blemish (Exodus 12:5)

10. False. The lamb had to be a male in the first year (Exodus 12:5)

Quiz 18

1. D. Sheep or goat (Exodus 12:5)

2. C. The fourteenth day (Exodus 12:6)

3. C. In the evening (Exodus 12:6)

4. C. On their houses' two doorposts and lintel (Exodus 12:7)

5. D. It was roasted (Exodus 12:8)

6. False. They were to eat the lamb with unleavened bread and bitter herbs (Exodus 12:8)

7. D. Burn (Exodus 12:10)

8. True (Exodus 12:11)

9. A. The Lord's Passover (Exodus 12:11)

10. A. In haste (Exodus 12:11)

Quiz 19

1. C. The gods of Egypt (Exodus12:12)

2. False. The Lord will pass over (Exodus 12:13)

3. C. Seven days (Exodus 12:15)

4. A. Leaven (Exodus 12:15)

5. C. Will be cut off (Exodus 12:15)

6. B. A holy convocation (Exodus 12:16)

7. B. Strangers or natives of the land (Exodus 12:19)

8. False. It is called the Passover lamb (Exodus 12:21)

9. D. Bowed their heads and worshiped (Exodus 12:27)

10. Here's how I'm thinking. Inside those houses were murders, thieves, liars, complainers, disobedient kids, Korah and his group who rebelled against Moses, etc. The people inside were not worthy of God's mercy, so God looked at the blood only. It is the same for us today. We are not worthy of being called the Children of God, but God has given us His Only Begotten Son's blood. That means, whenever He sees the blood on us, He sees His Sinless Son. That way, we become His own sons, daughters, and heirs of His Kingdom. Hallelujah to the Lord God!

Quiz 20

1. A. They should bless him, as well (Exodus 12:32).

2. B. Succoth (Exodus 12:37)

3. C. Six hundred thousand men (Exodus 12:37)

4. You have to ask questions about God and His activities in your parents' lives. God always wants us to remember what He has done for us. Asking your parents questions will help them remember what God has done for them. You have the right to ask your parents about their faith, and it's' their responsibility to tell you, as seen in Exodus 13:14. You need to know the reason they ask you to pray, read your Bible, go to church, etc. It is a collective responsibility (teamwork) to bring to memory what God has done in the Bible and what He has done for your parents. It helps build your confidence and faith in God. How awesome!

5. D. They were driven out of Egypt and could not wait, nor did they prepare provisions for themselves (Exodus 12:39).

6. B. Four hundred and thirty years (Exodus 12:40)

7. D. Every man's servant that is bought with money and is circumcised (Exodus 12:44)

8. B. They shall break none of its bones and shall take none of its flesh outside (Exodus 12:46)

9. True (Exodus 13:3-10)

10. C. Both man and beast (Exodus 13:12-13)

Quiz 21

1. C. They shall redeem them with a lamb (Exodus 13:13).

2. C. The male shall be the Lord's (Exodus 13:12).

3. B. They shall break its neck. Exodus 13:13

4. B. The house of bondage (Exodus 13:14).

5. B. When Pharaoh refused to let them go from Egypt, the Lord killed their firstborn of man and beast (Exodus 13:15).

6. A. The people might go back to Egypt if they saw war (Exodus 13:17)

7. True (Exodus 13:19)

8. A. Etham (Exodus 13:20)

9. A. The edge of the wilderness (Exodus 13:20)

10. A. Cloud (Exodus 13:21)

Quiz 22

1. False. By night, the Lord went before them in a pilar of fire (Exodus 13:21)

2. C. To give them light so they could travel day and night (Exodus 13:21)

3. C. Pi Hahiroth (Exodus 14:2)

4. A. The sea (Exodus 14:2)

5. A. Baal Zephon (Exodus 14:2)

6. C. Six hundred (Exodus 14:7)

7. False. The Children of Israel left with boldness Exodus 14:8

8. D. Did you bring us to die in the wilderness because there are no graves in Egypt? (Exodus 1411)

9. A. Didn't we ask you to leave us in Egypt so we can serve Pharoah? (Exodus 14:12)

10. B. Do not be afraid. Stand still and see the salvation of the Lord, which He will accomplish for you today (Exodus 14:13)

Quiz 23

1. D. The Egyptians you see today, you shall see them no more (Exodus 14:13).

2. D. The Lord will fight for you, and you shall hold your peace (Exodus 14:14).

3. A. Go forward (Exodus 14:15).

4. Apparently, after Moses stilled the people, he started crying out (praying) to God for deliverance. He had just faithfully proclaimed his faith in God aloud to the people, but Moses desperately prayed that God might do something. Moses should have quit praying and started acting in faith according to his pronouncements.

This is the same with us Christians today. We pray about things that God has empowered us to do, yet we still pray to God to do those things for us. In James 4:7, God asks us to "Resist the devil, and he will flee from us," yet we are always praying for God to remove Satan from our backs. You and I have power as a child of God, and I pray we would realize what God has done for us and use it to our advantage, in Jesus' name. Amen!

5. B. Stretch out his hand over the sea and divide it (Exodus14:16)

6. A. The Children of Israel were able to cross the sea on dry ground (Exodus 14:16)

7. D. So there will be a distance between them Exodus 14:20

8. A. East wind (Exodus 14:21)

9. False. The water was a wall to them on both sides (Exodus 14:22)

10. D. The pillar of cloud and fire (Exodus 14:24)

Quiz 24

1. C. He took their chariot's wheels off (Exodus 14:24).

2. A. Run away from Israel's face, for the Lord fights for His people and against Egypt (Exodus 14:25).

3. B. Stretch out his hand over the sea (Exodus 14:26).

4. C. Believed Him and His servant Moses (Exodus 14:31)

5. B. Sang unto the Lord (Exodus 15:1)

6. A. Gloriously (Exodus 15:1)

7. C. Song (Exodus 15:2)

8. D. Salvation (Exodus 15:2)

9. B. Praise Him (Exodus 15:2)

10. A. Exalt Him (Exodus 15:2)

Quiz 25

1. A. War (Exodus 15:3)

2. D. Glorious in power (Exodus 15:6)

3. C. The enemy in pieces (Exodus 15:6)

4. C. You (Exodus 15:7)

5. A. Wrath (Exodus 15:7)

6. D. Stubble (Exodus 15:7)

7. B. Nostrils (Exodus 15:8)

8. A. Together (Exodus 15:8)

9. A. Pursue, overtake (Exodus 15:9)

10. D. You, gods (Exodus 15:11)

Quiz 26

1. A. Holiness, praises, wonders (Exodus 15:11)

2. B. Prophetess (Exodus 15:20)

3. False. They all took timbrels (Exodus 15:20)

4. B. Shur (Exodus 15:22)

5. B. Three days (Exodus 15:22)

6. A. Water (Exodus 15:22)

7. A. Marah (Exodus 15:23)

8. B. The water was bitter (Exodus 15:23)

9. C. A tree (Exodus 15:25)

10. B. Heals them (Exodus 15:26)

Quiz 27

1. Moses was God-dependent. He always cried (prayed) and waited on God for answers. In Exodus 15:25, Moses cried to God, and He showed him a tree to throw into the water to make it drinkable. In Exodus 17: 2-7, the people complained and tempted God because they were thirsty, so Moses cried to God, and He told him to take some elders to the rock in Horeb and that He would stand on top of it. Moses was to strike the rock, and water was to come out of it. (More examples here - Numbers 11:10-23; 12:13, Leviticus 24:10-13).

2. B. Elim (Exodus 15:27)

3. B. The wilderness of Sin (Exodus 16:1)

4. False. The wilderness of Sin is between Elim and Sinai (Exodus 16:1)

5. D. Fifteenth (Exodus 16:1)

6. D. Hunger (Exodus 16:3)

7. D. Heaven (Exodus 16:4)

8. D. Sixth (Exodus 16:5)

9. C. The glory of the Lord (Exodus 16:7)

10. B. Bread, meat (Exodus 16:8)

Quiz 28

1. A. The glory of God in the cloud (Exodus 16:10)

2. B. Quails (Exodus 16:13)

3. C. Manna (Exodus 16:35)

4. D. It bred worms and stank (Exodus 16:20)

5. B. Melted (Exodus 16:21)

6. False. The seventh day was called the Sabbath day (Exodus 16:23)

7. B. Wafers made with honey (Exodus 16:31)

8. B. Forty years (Exodus 16:35)

9. D. Rephidim (Exodus 17:1)

10. B. Horeb (Exodus 17:6)

Quiz 29

1. A. Massah and Meribah (Exodus 17:7)

2. The manna the Children of Israel ate daily would stink and breed worms when the sun rose, except on Sabbath days. But the manna Aaron kept in a pot was preserved for a long time without that problem (Exodus 16:20, 34).

3. He kept them in a golden pot.

4. False. The Amalekites came to fight against Israel (Exodus 17:8)

5. A. Joshua (Exodus 17:9)

6. C. Aaron and Hur (Exodus 17:10)

7. B. A stone (Exodus 17:12)

8. B. The-Lord-Is-My-Banner (Exodus 17:15)

9. A. It symbolizes how Jesus became living water for us (John 4:10-11 and 7:38).

10. C. The Mountain of God (Exodus 18:1-5)

Quiz 30

1. D. Burnt offering (Exodus 18:12)

2. A. True (Exodus 18:12)

3. C. Jethro (Exodus 18:17-24)

4. D. Wilderness of Sinai (Exodus 19:1)

5. A. Before the mountain (Exodus 19:2)

6. C. He bore them on eagle's wings (Exodus 19:4)

7. A. A kingdom of priests and a holy nation (Exodus 19:6)

8. D. All that the Lord has said, we will do (Exodus 19:8)

9. B. Third (Exodus 19:11)

10. C. Stoned or shot with an arrow (Exodus 19:13)

Quiz 31

1. B. Smoke Exodus (19:16-18)

2. The miracle of manna God provided every morning for the Israelites, except on the Sabbath, during their forty years in the wilderness, is the longest recorded miracle (Exodus 16:35)

3. A. Because the Lord descended upon it in fire (Exodus 19:18)

4. A. It quaked (Exodus 19:18)

5. False. The Lord answered Moses with a voice (Exodus 19:19)

6. A. Aaron (Exodus 19:24)

7. B. Believe Moses forever

8. A. You shall have no other gods before Me (Exodus 20:3)

9. C. He is a jealous God (Exodus 20:5)

10. B. You shall not make for yourselves a carved image. You shall not bow down to them nor serve them (Exodus 20:4)

Quiz 32

1. He spoke of the New Covenant we now have in Christ. Jesus died to redeem us from the law's curse (Galatians 3:13).

2. C. You shall not take the name of the Lord your God in vain (Exodus 20:7).

3. C. Remember the Sabbath day and keep it holy (Exodus 20:8).

4. A. Honor your father and mother (Exodus 20:12).

5. A. You shall not kill (Exodus 20:13).

6. B. You shall not commit adultery (Exodus 20:14).

7. C. You shall not steal (Exodus 20:15)

8. B. You shall not bear false witness against your neighbor (Exodus 20:16).

9. D. You shall not covet your neighbor's wife or house (Exodus 20:17).

10. The new commandment is for us to LOVE one another, as Jesus has loved us (John 13:34). Love is referred to as "The fulfillment of the law" (Romans 13:8-11), and it is also called "The Royal Law" (James 2:8).

Quiz 33

1. B. They will die. Exodus (20:18-19)

2. False. The Lord has come to test them (Exodus 20:20)

3. A. Burnt and peace offerings (Exodus 20:24)

4. C. Six years (Exodus 21:2)

5. C. The children shall belong to the master (Exodus 21:3-4).

6. True (Exodus 21:12)

7. D. Killed (Exodus 21:15)

8. D. Killed (Exodus 21:16)

9. True (Exodus 21:17)

10. B. Punished (Exodus 21:20)

Quiz 34

1. Had eaten of the old corn in the Land of Canaan (Joshua 5:12).

2. A. Life for life, eye for an eye, tooth for tooth, hand for hand, foot for foot, burn for burn, wound for wound, and stripe for stripe (Exodus 21:22-25)

3. C. Let them go free (Exodus 21:26)

4. True (Exodus 21:28)

5. C. He shall be acquitted (Exodus 21:28)

6. C. Give the owner of the dead animal money, and the dead one shall be his (Exodus 21:33-34).

7. A. They shall share the proceeds (Exodus 21:35)

8. C. Pay ox for ox. He shall take the dead one and give his ox to the owner of the dead ox (Exodus 21:36).

9. True (Exodus 22:1)

10. C. A thief breaking in (Exodus 22:2)

Quiz 35

1. A. Double (Exodus 22:4)

2. False. The thief shall be sold (Exodus 22:3)

3. B. A sorceress (Exodus 22:18)

4. B. Killed (Exodus 22:19)

5. False. Whoever sacrifices to other gods shall be destroyed (Exodus 22:20)

6. C. They were strangers in Egypt (Exodus 22:21)

7. C. Kill them with the sword; their wives shall be widows and their children, fatherless (Exodus 22:22-24)

8. B. Not collect interest (Exodus 22:25)

9. A. Curse (Exodus 22:28)

10. B. Seven, eight (Exodus 22:29-30)

Quiz 36

1. D. Throw it to the dogs (Exodus 22:31)

2. D. Circulate (Exodus 23:1)

3. D. Do evil (Exodus 23:2)

4. True (Exodus 23:3)

5. D. Take them back to the owner (Exodus 23:4)

6. Righteous (Exodus 23:7)

7. C. Justify (Exodus 23:7)

8. A. It blinds the discerning and perverts the words of the righteous (Exodus 23:8)

9. C. Six, one (Exodus 23:10-11)

10. A. So all that they have–animals and servants - may rest and be refreshed (Exodus 23:12)

Quiz 37

1. B. Three (Exodus 23:14)

2. D. Unleavened bread, Harvest, and Ingathering (Exodus 23:14-16)

3. Tempting the Lord means to doubt His presence and/or ability.

4. B. Bringing the firstfruits of their labors they have sown in the fields to the Lord (Exodus 23:16)

5. D. At the end of the year (Exodus 23:16)

6. C. A. Males (Exodus 23:17)

7. His name is in Him (Exodus 23:20-21)

8. D. Enemy and adversary (Exodus 23:22)

9. Bow down (Exodus 23:23-24)

10. The Amalekites were the descendants of Esau (Genesis 36:12 and 15-16) and, therefore, relatives of the Israelites.

Quiz 38

1. They attacked the weak and weary people at the back of the camp (Deuteronomy 25:17-20).

2. D. Sickness (Exodus 23:25)

3. B. Fulfill the number of their days (Exodus 23:26)

4. C. The land will become desolate, and the beast of the land will increase (Exodus 23:27-29).

5. B. Make covenants (Exodus 23:31-32)

6. B. They will sin against Him by serving their gods and will be a snare to them (Exodus 23:32-33)

7. D. The elders (Exodus 24:1)

8. A. Moses (Exodus 24:2)

9. C. According to the tribes (sons) of Israel (Exodus 24:3-4)

10. D. An Oxen (Exodus 24:5)

Quiz 39

1. Under the New Covenant, God's promises for us aren't dependent on our obedience or holiness to hundreds of commandments, as in the Old Testament. Everything has been made available to us through faith in Christ (Romans 3:28 and Galatians 2:16).

2. C. The Book of the Covenant (Exodus 24:6-7)

3. D. This is the blood of the covenant which the Lord has made with you according to all these words (Exodus 24:7-8).

4. A. A pave work of sapphire stone like the very heavens in its clarity (Exodus 24:10).

5. B. Ate and drank (Exodus 24:11)

6. A. God invited him (Exodus 24:12)

7. D. Joshua (Exodus 24:13)

8. False. Joshua was an assistant (Exodus 24:13)

9. C. Aaron, Hur (Exodus 24:14)

10. A. Cloud (Exodus 24:15)

Quiz 40

1. B. Six days (Exodus 24:16)

2. A. A consuming fire (Exodus 24:17)

3. False. Moses was there for forty days and nights (Exodus 24:18)

4. C. Anyone who is willing with his heart only (Exodus 25:2)

5. C. Logs of wood, axes, and livestock (Exodus 25:3-5)

6. A. For light (Exodus 25:6)

7. For the anointing oil and the sweet incense (Exodus 25:6)

8. They were consulted when they wanted to inquire of the Lord.

In First Samuel 28:6, Saul inquired of the Lord, and He did not answer him by Urim or by dreams. In Nehemiah 7:65, the governor advised the people not to eat from the most holy things until a priest showed up with Urim and Thummim. David used the ephod that contained the Urim and Thummim in 1 Samuel 30:7-8.

9. C. Build Him a sanctuary (Exodus 25:8-9).

10. B. So He could dwell among them (Exodus 25:8)

Quiz 41

1. B. He showed him (Exodus 25:9).

2. False. They shall make an ark of Acacia wood (Exodus 25:10)

3. A. Two and a half cubits (Exodus 25:10)

4. B. A cubit and half (Exodus 25:10)

5. C. Pure gold (Exodus 25:11)

6. True (Exodus 25:11)

7. It symbolizes the transference of their sins to the animal. The animal has to die because the wages of sin is death (Romans 6:23). That was for the Old Testament believer. We are free from that. Hallelujah! All our sins have been placed on Jesus, and He is the atoning sacrifice for the entire world (1 John 2:2). The sins of the Old Covenant believers were atoned for temporarily, but our sins have been atoned for forever! Praise God!

8. B. The four corners (Exodus 25:12)

9. B. Gold (Exodus 25:13)

10. D. Into the rings (Exodus 25:14)

Quiz 42

1. C. So they can easily carry them around (Exodus: 25:14).

2. A. The testimony (Exodus 25:16)

3. A. Pure gold (Exodus 25:17)

4. False. The length shall be two and a half cubits (Exodus 25:17)

5. B. One and a half cubit (Exodus 25:17)

6. D. Two (Exodus 25:18)

7. B. Two ends of the mercy seat (Exodus 25:18)

8. D. Face each other (Exodus 25:20)

9. True (Exodus 25:21)

10. This account underscores the humility of Moses. Moses was not selfish, and he didn't care about the personal advantage this opportunity would have brought to him. Instead, he interceded for them. The Bible says in Numbers 12:3, "Now the man Moses was very humble, more than all men who were on the face of the earth."

Quiz 43

1. C. Two cubits (Exodus 25:22)

2. A. One cubit (Exodus 25:23)

3. B. One-and-a-half-cubit (Exodus 25:23)

4. B. They are holders for the poles to bear the table (Exodus 25:27)

5. A. Dishes, pans, pitchers, and bowls (Exodus 25:29)

6. C. Hammered work (Exodus 25:31)

7. D. Six (Exodus 25:32)

8. B. Ten (Exodus 26:1)

9. False. The colors shall be blue, purple, and scarlet (Exodus 25:1)

Quiz 44

1. A. Twenty-eight (Exodus 26:2)

2. D. Four cubits (Exodus 26:2)

3. C. Five six (Exodus 26:3)

4. False. They shall make loops of blue (Exodus 26:4)

5. B. Fifty (Exodus 26:5)

6. C. Gold (Exodus 26:5-6)

7. A. Goat hair (Exodus 26:7)

8. A. Eleven (Exodus 26:7)

9. B. Thirty cubits (Exodus 26:8)

10. A. Four cubits (Exodus 26:8)

Quiz 45

1. King Solomon built the temple, and the priest could not go into the temple to minister because the cloud, the glory of God, had filled the House of the Lord (1 Kings 8:11 and 2 Chronicles 5:14).

2. C. Bronze (Exodus 26:9-11)

3. B. Ram skins (Exodus 26:14)

4. False, the ram skin shall be dyed red (Exodus 26:14)

5. C. Badger skins (Exodus 26:14)

6. A. Acacia wood (Exodus 26:15)

7. D. Forty (Exodus 26:18-21)

8. B. Twenty on the south and twenty on the north Exodus: 26:18-21

9. A. Square (Exodus 27:1)

10. False. The height shall be three cubits (Exodus 27:1)

Quiz 46

1. B. Bronze (Exodus 27:2)

2. B. To receive its ashes (Exodus 27:3)

3. B. Bronze (Exodus 27:3)

4. D. Olive Exodus: 27:20

5. D. Aaron and his sons (Exodus 27:21)

6. A. Aaron and his sons (Exodus 28:1)

7. True (Exodus 28:2)

8. C. The spirit of wisdom (Exodus 28:3-4)

9. A. Artistically (Exodus 28:6)

10. B. The names of the Children of Israel (Jacob) (Exodus 28:10)

Quiz 47

1. B. From oldest to youngest (Exodus 28:9-11)

2. False. Aaron shall bear the engraved names on his shoulder before the Lord (Exodus 28:12)

3. D. Blue (Exodus 28:31)

4. A. Holiness to the Lord (Exodus 28:36).

5. A. Wheat (Exodus 29:1-2)

6. The presence of the Lord. When it moved, the Israelites moved. If the Lord (cloud) stayed, they stayed.

7. D. Wash them with water (Exodus 29:4).

8. A. Perpetual statute (Exodus 29:9)

9. D. They shall put their hand on top of its heads as Moses kills it (Exodus 29:10).

10. C. A sin-offering (Exodus 29:14)

Quiz 48

1. A. Burnt (Exodus 29:18)

2. True (Exodus 29:18)

3. D. A ram of consecration (Exodus 29:22)

4. D. A wave offering (Exodus 29:24)

5. A. A burnt offering (Exodus 29:25)

6. C. A wave offering (Exodus 29:26)

7. D. Aaron's sons (Exodus 29:29)

8. False. Aaron's replacement shall wear his garments for seven (Exodus 29:30)

9. A. Aaron and his sons (Exodus 29:31-32)

10. C. To consecrate and sanctify them (Exodus 29:33)

Quiz 49

1. B. They shall be burned with fire (Exodus 29:34).

2. B. Seven days (Exodus 29:35)

3. C. Sin-offering (Exodus 29:36)

4. A. Holy (Exodus 29:37)

5. B. Twice (Exodus 29:38-39)

6. False. Moses was the use lambs of the first year (Exodus 29:38)

7. B. Grain and drink offering (Exodus 29:39-41)

8. B. Two (Exodus 30:2)

9. A. Gold (Exodus 30:3)

10. B. Aaron (Exodus 30:7)

Quiz 50

1. B. Two (Exodus 30:7-8)

2. The priest was to wear linen to keep them from sweating (Ezekiel 44:18).

3. C. Drink offerings (Exodus 30:9)

4. True (Exodus 30:10)

5. D. Being plagued (Exodus 30:11-12)

6. B. Twenty years (Exodus 30:14)

7. B. Water (Exodus 30:18)

8. A. Aaron and his sons (Exodus 30:19)

9. D. They will die (Exodus 30:20)

10. D. Holy anointing oil (Exodus 30:22-25)

Quiz 51

1. C. Cut off from his people (Exodus 30:31-33)

2. A. ut off Exodus (30:34-38)

3. D. Bezalel (Exodus 31:2)

4. C. Uri (Exodus 31:2)

5. C. Judah (Exodus 31:2)

6. B. Wisdom (Exodus 31:3)

7. A. Aholiab (Exodus 31:6)

8. D. Dan (Exodus 31:6)

9. True (Exodus 31:14)

10. A. Two tablets of the Testimony (Exodus 31:18)

Quiz 52

1. C. Commandments

2. C. God (Exodus 31:18)

3. False. He wrote on it with His finger (Exodus 31:18)

4. God (Exodus 25:2).

5. D. Aaron (Exodus 32:1)

6. B. Golden earrings (Exodus 32:2)

7. D. A calf (Exodus 32:4)

8. True Exodus 32:5

9. D. Offered a burnt offering (Exodus 32:6)

10. B. Pleaded with God for the Israelites (Exodus 32:7-12)

Quiz 53

1. D. Abraham, Isaac, and Jacob (Exodus 32:13)

2. C. Joshua (Exodus 32:17)

3. A. He broke them at the foot of the mountain as he cast them down (Exodus 32:19)

4. B. Drink from it (Exodus 32:20)

5. D. Levi Exodus (32:25-26)

6. B. About three thousand (Exodus 32:28)

7. B. Blot him out of the book He has written (Exodus 32:32)

8. A. Whoever has sinned against Me, I will blot him out of My book (Exodus 32:33)

9. B. Take off their ornaments (Exodus 33:4-6)

10. False. Moses called it the Tabernacle of Meeting (Exodus 33:7)

Quiz 54

1. C. Stand in front of their tents and watch Moses until he enters the tabernacle (Exodus 33:7-9)

2. B. A pillar of cloud descended and stood at the door of the tabernacle, and the Lord talked with Moses (Exodus 33:9).

3. B. Worship each man in his tent (Exodus 33:9-10).

4. C. He spoke to him face to face, as a man speaks to his friend (Exodus 33:11).

5. True (Exodus 33:11)

6. A. Nun (Exodus 33:11)

7. B. He knows him by name (Exodus 33:12).

8. D. His people (Exodus 33:12-13)

9. C. Do not remove us from here if Your presence will not go with us (Exodus 33:15)

10. B. Show him His glory (Exodus 33:18).

Quiz 55

1. A. That he cannot see His face; for no man shall see Him and live (Exodus 33:20).

2. D. His back (Exodus 33:23)

3. B. Mount Sinai (Exodus 34:2)

4. C. Lest the inhabitants be snares in their midst (Exodus 34:10-12)

5. C. Jealous God (Exodus 34:14)

6. C. Throughout the entire year, even during the plowing and harvest seasons (Exodus 34:21)

7. A. Forty days (Exodus 34:28)

8. C. Shone (Exodus 34:29-30)

9. False. They were scared (Exodus 34:30).

10. C. Veiled himself (Exodus 34:31-35)

Quiz 56

1. A. Killed (Exodus 35:2)

2. The testimony is the two tablets inscribed with the Ten Commandments.

3. A. People whose heart was stirred and those whose spirit was willing (Exodus 35:21)

4. D. The rulers (Exodus 35:27)

5. A. A freewill offering (Exodus 35:29)

6. B. He blessed the people.

7. A. On the first day of the first month (Exodus 40:2)

8. B. Second

9. A. The glory of the Lord filled it (Exodus 40:34-35).

10. C. He was not able to go into the tabernacle (Exodus 40:34-35).

11. True (Exodus 40:35-38)

12. The veil symbolizes Jesus. It was torn in two, from top to bottom, at the death of our Lord Jesus Christ (Mathew 27:51 and Mark 15:38), symbolizing that the separation between God and man was removed. Hallelujah! We now have a new living way to approach the Father through the veil: Jesus (Hebrew 10:20).

Resources

Youversion. (1996). [Computer software]. Life Church. https://www.youversion.com/the-bible-app/

About Author

"Only One Life" writes with a heart to help children know and love God from an early age. Through simple stories and biblical truths, their books give parents and teachers tools to guide children toward faith in Jesus and a strong foundation that will last a lifetime. Each story is written to spark imagination, open conversation, and lead young readers closer to the God who loves them.

Learn, grow, and love God together...

Also By Only One Life

Biblical Bedtime Stories for Kids: Old Testament Amazing Moments Pointing Your Children to God, Ages 4 – 8.
Biblical Bedtime Stories for Kids: 113 Old Testament Amazing Moments Pointing Your Children to God Coloring Book, Ages 4 – 8.
Biblical Questions and Answers for Smart Kids: Quizzes Focused on the Book of Genesis to Help Your Children Grow and Learn about God – Who He is, His Love, and His Relationship with Humanity.
Biblical Characters for Kids: Adventures of the Patriarchs God Wants Your Children to Know, Ages 7-12.
Biblical Bedtime Stories for Kids: New Testament Amazing Moments Pointing Your Children to God, Ages 4 – 8.
Biblical Bedtime Stories for Kids: Old Testament Amazing Moments Pointing Your Children to God Coloring Book, Ages 4 – 8.
Biblical Food for Kids: 91 Daily Nutritious Wholesome Meal for Raising Healthy and Spirit-Filled Children to Giants, Ages 7-12. (Bible Meal Plan Book 1)